Toronto by G

The Night Hawks o

As Seen by the Reporters of

"The Toronto News"

Toronto News

Alpha Editions

This edition published in 2024

ISBN : 9789357968683

Design and Setting By
Alpha Editions
www.alphaedis.com
Email - info@alphaedis.com

INTRODUCTION.

Night has fallen over the city. The hum of a hundred industries which make the daytime resonant with the whirr of wheels, the clank of hammers, and the throb of huge engines, is silent. Deserted are the factories and workshops and warehouses, where a few hours ago all was life and stir in the eager struggle for subsistence. The great arteries of the city's traffic still present a scene of animation. The stores are yet open, and crowds, partly on business, partly on pleasure bent, throng the sidewalks—standing densely packed at intervals round the store of some tradesman more enterprising than his fellows, who displays amid a blaze of light, some novel device to arrest the attention and tickle the fancy of the passer-by. Workingmen and their wives, evidently out on a shopping expedition, pass from one store to another in search of bargains. Pleasure-seekers, bound for the different places of amusement, whirl past in hacks or dismount from the humble and more economical street-car. But the element which largely out-numbers all others is that of young men and girls out for an evening stroll. Up and down Yonge street they pass in parties of two and three, with frequent interchange of chaff and banter, not always of the most refined order. There is a general aimlessness in their demeanor as they slowly saunter along arm-in-arm, frequently occupying the whole sidewalk, to the great annoyance of more active pedestrians. The young fellows are mostly smoking pipes or cheap cigars and talking loudly to their companions. Occasionally they stop for a bit of horse-play, pushing and wrestling with each other. Now the "masher" is in all his glory. It is not often that any self-respecting girl who goes on her way quietly is accosted, but any lightness of demeanor on the part of a young woman alone on the street is pretty certain to expose her to the attentions of some lounger bedecked with cheap jewelry, who prides himself on his fascinating powers and has an ever-ready "Good evening, miss!" for any member of the fair sex not positively bad-looking, whose appearance gives him courage to make an approach.

THE MASHER

is of all ages and stations. It is only the more reckless and less experienced who venture to accost a stranger on the street without a reasonable excuse. The old hands at the business who occupy respectable positions in society generally assume a previous acquaintance, and if their advances are not favorably received there is the ready excuse of mistaken identity, "I really beg your pardon, I took you for Miss So-and-So," etc., and exit under cover of profuse apologies.

During the earlier hours of the evening there are kaleidoscopic changes of scene. Sensations of all kinds draw the crowd hither and thither. An arrest, an alarm of fire, with the rush of the engines and hook and ladder wagons tearing like mad through the streets, a march out of the volunteers with the inspiriting martial music of the band—any of these distractions sift out the younger and more excitable element, who follow at the top of their speed, leaving the streets half deserted. There is nothing delights the rougher element more than to see an unfortunate who has been imbibing too freely "run in." A blue coat in charge of anybody in fact always draws, particularly if the delinquent is noisy and obstreperous. And a fire is a thing of beauty and a joy forever. At the first alarm the saunterers are all animation. "Where is it?" is the question on everyone's tongue, and as soon as the locality is defined, away they go—fortunate if they arrive before the firemen cease playing, for under the fire alarm system a conflagration has very little opportunity of making headway.

Of late the Salvation Army is a frequent element in diversifying the life of the streets after nightfall. Its parades invariably attract a crowd of strollers, many of them of a class whom the ministrations of the regular religious bodies do not reach. Their banners and uniform, their marching music, and the stentorian voices of their street preachers have by this time become a recognized and familiar feature of city life, and though the novelty of their advent has worn off the people manifest as much interest as ever in their sayings and doings. Their parade in the middle of the street is accompanied by simultaneous parallel processions of a less orderly character on the sidewalks. Whatever may be thought of the ultimate effect of this manner of presenting religion to the mass, there is no question that it arrests their attention.

As the night advances, the crowd thins out.

THE STREET-LOUNGERS,

male and female, disappear one by one, the stores have closed their doors, until the only places which show signs of business activity are here and there a saloon or a tobacco store, which may or may not have a keg of lager on tap in the back-room or a "little game" upstairs. Now the streets again assume for a few minutes a lively aspect as the places of amusement are emptied of their audiences. Overladen street cars make their final trips, toiling wearily up the ascent with frequent stoppages as the suburbs are neared. And now the streets are almost deserted again. Stray pedestrians hurry or totter homeward. The saloon lights are extinguished, but acute ears can still hear the clink of glasses and the subdued conversation of groups of revellers who are bound to make a night of it, and are cheerfully fuddling themselves in a back room. The wearied bar-keeper will let them out by a side door in an hour or two. He will breathe a heartfelt sigh of relief as they stumble over the threshold, and slipping the bolt with alacrity, to prevent any other belated seeker after the ardent gaining entrance, he will knock down about half of the cash the party have left, and congratulate himself on his honesty in leaving so much for his employer.

One o'clock. The city sleeps. The few stragglers on the streets only serve to make the general impression of silence and solitude the more vivid by contrast. Here and there is a pedestrian on his homeward way, or perhaps a party of two or three late roysterers laughing and bursting into snatches of song, but growing suddenly silent and bracing up as the measured tread of the blue-coated guardian of the night approaches. Now and then a stray hack rumbles by, the noise of the wheels gradually dying away in the distance and leaving no other sound audible. The night watchman passes, carefully trying the doors of the stores and halting for a friendly chat with the policeman on the corner of the block. The puffing of the locomotive or steamboat engine a mile or two away, inaudible during the day-time, sounds strangely near. Up and down the long stretches of sidewalk hardly anyone is in sight. It is like a city of the dead. The cold steely-blue brilliancy of the electric light makes the darkness around their radiant circle seem denser and throws the dark shadows of intervening objects across the street. The long rows of gas-lamps on the side streets "pale their ineffectual fires" and present but a sickly glimmer by contrast, and overhead shine the eternal stars, whose distant scintillations amid the silence and darkness of midnight have ever had power to speak from the soul of things to the soul of man, and suggest the ever-old yet ever-new problems of life and destiny unheard and unheeded amid the distractions of the day.

CHAPTER I.
THE TOILERS OF THE NIGHT.

When the streets leading from the center of the city are full of people hurrying gleefully or otherwise homewards from their day's toil, there is another small section of the community who are hurrying in the opposite direction. These men begin to work when all others have ceased. The morning newspaper employes, the telegraph operators, the bakers, the policemen, and the nightwatchmen are the most important divisions of these toilers of the night.

In connection with the different newspaper establishments in the city there are probably about 600 persons employed at night. These include compositors, pressmen, stereotypers, mailing clerks, editors, reporters, and route boys. All do not work during the same hours, but some portions of their various tasks are accomplished when "Night draws her sable mantle around and pins it with a star." The compositors begin "setting" about 7 o'clock and cease about 3. This does not comprise the whole of their work, however, as the next day they spend two or three hours filling up the cases which they did their best to empty the night before. It is an exceedingly see-saw business—undoing in the day what they performed in the night. The work is entirely by the piece, and a fast hand makes a good wage to reward him for his toil, but this wage represents twelve or thirteen hours of labor in the large establishments. Many of the men think that it would be better to

RESTRICT THE HOURS OF TOIL

to ten, as they claim that bosses don't look at the number of hours worked, but at the money earned. The hours of the literary staff of a morning paper are fitful and uncertain, but the general rule is that when you are awake you had better go to work. The stereotypers get to their cauldrons of boiling lead shortly after midnight, and the pressmen are at their post about 3.30—just when the typo is washing his hands and preparing to leave. The mailing clerks are the next to put in an appearance, and almost simultaneously the little route-boy slips through the door, prepared for his morning tramp.

About sixty-five policemen hold watch over the sleeping city by night. Their work varies in winter and summer. Just now they remain on beat eight hours at a stretch. In winter they are on three hours, off three hours, and on again for the same length of time. Their work and its incidents will form the topic of another of these sketches.

The next most important body of men, and probably more numerous, is the bakers. It is calculated that about 300 persons find employment in supplying our citizens with their bread. All of these, however, do not work at night.

Their labor begins about three o'clock, and they may be seen about that hour in their floury garments hieing them to their shops. Their work is performed in very hot rooms, and is on the whole

LABORIOUS AND MONOTONOUS.

On their skill depends one of the greatest luxuries of the table—a well baked loaf of bread—and to their credit be it said, success very frequently crowns their efforts.

The telegraph operators who work at night do not average over a dozen men. This staff is lessened or increased very much in sympathy with the quantity of dispatches which are coming in to the morning papers. When any great event is transpiring in another land or another part of this country, and long messages are coming in concerning it, the staff has to be increased, and for this purpose men are drafted from the day staff. It is an unhealthy business. In most mortality-tables, the life of the operator shows the shortest average. Not long ago they struck for higher wages and made a plucky fight, but monopoly was too much for them. Ever since they have had the screws put on them pretty tightly. Reductions in the staff and reductions in the salaries have been the order of the day. In view of these facts some of them think that it is a good thing they don't live too long.

These are briefly the main facts connected with the toilers of the night, men who work while the rest of the world are asleep—asleep feeling assured that the telegrapher is gathering in for them the news of the world, and that the newspaper men are printing it for them, that the baker is preparing for them the breakfast roll, and that the policeman is watching over their lives and their property, and keeping his weather eye on those other people of the night, whom we are pleased to designate the Hawks.

CHAPTER II.
AN ALL-NIGHT EATING HOUSE.

The classes about whom we have been speaking take dinner at midnight, and for some of them at least, the eating house which keeps open till early morning is indeed a boon. It cannot be decried therefore even though it be a fact that the night hawks are accommodated thereby. Some of these places keep open later than others, but, as far as I know, without exception they are all situated on York street, and are a pleasant substitute for the whiskey dens which used to flourish there. A series of visits paid to these places showed that very few of the customers belonged to the class of toilers. The prowlers of all ranks and degrees though were well represented. The room is generally apportioned into little stalls curtained off from the room. It is a common saying that adversity makes strange bed-fellows, but granting that that is so, it may also be affirmed that liquor makes strange companions. In one of these eating houses one night there was observed in one compartment a doctor, a lion-tamer and a tailor, all on first-rate terms; in another was observed a commercial traveler, an Irish navvy and a tramp printer, all insisting on

SPEAKING AT THE SAME TIME

regarding their travels, not so harmonious; in another were banqueting three "colored pussons" discussing whether Bob Berry was not a greater oarsman than Hanlan. The only regret experienced by the onlooker was that he could not sprinkle the "coons" among the other feasters and thus render the melange complete. In another room a couple of gentlemen were seated who had been seen on more than one occasion in the police court explaining how it was that they came to be in a room where a faro lay-out was also found. These gentry were faring high, as the bottled beer beside them showed. Dame Fortune had probably smiled on them and now they were "smiling" back at her.

Oysters are very well in season, but the standard, substantial and favorite dish at the all-night eating house is the platter of pork and beans. To the hungry gentleman, who has probably missed his six o'clock meal, this dish is a reviver of a distinctly perceptible kind. That man whom you saw skip out just now came in with a weary step, but you now see the result of his mess of lentils and swine flesh. He steps out as briskly as a young giant refreshed with wine.

One of the most interesting characters I met with during these visits was a shabby genteel party, who came in about one in the morning and occupied a seat at the table at which I sat. I purposely delayed my meal to observe this specimen. The way in which he chose and ordered his viands from the rather limited bill of fare, showed an acquaintance of an earlier day with Jewell &

Clow, or some other swell restaurant. His garments were a study. They were beautifully preserved, and really looked much younger than their years. His collar, tie and cuffs were not, as some lesser humorist has remarked before,

PRIMA FACIE EVIDENCE OF A SHIRT.

A ring on his little finger would probably have brought five cents at a second-hand dealers, but it was chosen with such taste that it might well pass for "a ring, sir, that my father secured among the loot taken at the fall of Delhi." A piece of black ribbon was twisted in one of the button-holes of his vest, but an unfortunate accident with his fork flipped out the door-key that was attached to the other end of it.

"That's rather a novel thing, sir," he said to me.

"Yes," I said, somewhat vaguely, thinking that he alluded to the deception involved.

"I thought that was a clever thing when the idea first struck me. Frequently in changing my dress of an evening I forgot to transfer my latch-key from one pocket to the other, and the consequence was that I was put to the annoyance of waking up my landlady at an unseemly hour. The last occasion I had to do this I took out my repeater to see what the hour was and the thought struck me that if I had my key instead of my watch there would be no trouble. That was enough. I told my landlady my idea and she thought it was capital, and offered to keep my watch safe for me. I have worn the key thus ever since. I am not so particular what time I reach my lodgings, as to be sure of getting in there when I do."

My communicative vis-a-vis was feeding very heartily during this interesting conversation. He went on to speak of the Egyptian war and showed with his knife the exact position of General Gordon, and explained lucidly and to his own entire satisfaction how the venturesome Englishman could be rescued very easily, with a comparatively trifling expenditure of

BLOOD AND TREASURE.

This last was a favorite phrase, and he rolled it unctuously over his tongue when his beans ran out. But his vivacity was evidently on the wane, and he rose with a tinge of humility in his manner. He approached the landlord and whispered something. That individual, however, did not answer with a whisper, but said, with fair power of lungs, "Oh, that be d—d for a yarn. Fork over that quarter now, and no fooling." I could just hear my late comrade begin a sentence with "But, my dear sir," when the indignant restaurateur would break in, "My dear sir nothing; I want my money." With this he relieved his debtor of his hat, expressing his determination to keep it till he got paid. The shabby genteel one had furnished a subject for one of these sketches, and thinking that was worth something, I paid his shot and charged it to THE NEWS. He immediately became dignified again, recovered his hat, treated the landlord with cold disdain, and thanked me with a jaunty air, as if to say, "Old boy, you have helped me out of a little fix; I'll reciprocate some other time."

Poor devil, I saw him three hours after in an early opening bar, looking very sleepy and fagged. He had probably been walking the streets ever since I left him, and had taken refuge here in hopes that some fresh stranger would ask him to take a drink of that liquid for which he had bartered every comfort in life, and for which he will soon barter life itself. I did not ask him why he had omitted to use his ingenious key.

CHAPTER III.
THE CABMAN'S CHATTER.

Knowing that a hackman knew as much of city life if not more, than any other one man out of 10,000, I climbed on the box of a hack and asked an old-timer to drive me around town.

"All right boss, get up here and I'll drive you to the Queen's taste."

After some general conversation I drifted to the subject of what sights and sounds a hackman sees and hears after nightfall.

"I've seen too much of that to my own sorrow, as you know," my companion said. "If I had seen less of it, instead of being another man's servant, I would have had a carriage of my own. Not that there ain't more money to be made at night than in the day time if a man holds a good sharp rein on himself. A fellow that keeps his eye on the main chance and knows how to keep a stiff upper lip will make dollars and dollars."

"I suppose your work has given you a big insight into the wickedness of a great city."

"What I don't know of the blackguards, men and women, in this town ain't worth knowing. I am up to every scheme that has ever been tried, I believe. I tell you, we hackmen are about as fly as they make them."

"You can't all be extra 'fly,'" I said.

"Well, there are a lot of new fellows in the business, and they are regular chumps. It's them that spoils everything. They don't know the kind of men to strike for a good fat fare, and when they do they bungle it, and get themselves in the papers and give the hackmen a bad name. The business is overrun. Everybody that knows how to put on a horse-collar now wants to drive hack. They see that it is a job which there ain't any hard work in. But there's any amount of dirty work for us. We're out in all sorts of weather, sun and rain and frost. We're liable to be out till all hours of the night and up by daylight the next morning to catch a train. Then, if we want to make a cent, we have to do everything we're asked. It's quite a common snap to have a stranger come to you at the Union station and ask you to drive him up to one of them houses. Now, just look at such work as that—acting as a bad woman's directory. But I don't know of a hackman on the stand who won't take the job. You bet your life I make them fellows pay accordin' to a special tariff. Do you know, last summer I drove an old fellow from Parry Sound up to a house on Little Nelson street. When he paid me my fare I saw he had a big wad of bills. He told me to come back next day about two o'clock, as he wanted to be driven to a sister of his who lived on the Kingston road. I called for him next afternoon, but the old man was not ready to go, and would you believe, I called for that old tarrier for five days, and on the fifth day he didn't have a picayune. I had to drive him to Singer's pawn shop, where he put up his watch and chain for money enough to take him home. He never saw his sister, and I often wondered what yarn he told the folks at home about his visit to town."

"Do you suppose they robbed him?"

"Oh! not exactly robbed him, but I heard afterwards that the old fool was offering prizes of five dollar notes for whoever could kick highest. Do you know that if it wasn't for the strangers half of these places would have to shut their doors."

"I believe you are right."

"I know it. Why, the missuses of these places know that so well that a hackman who always takes such fares to her place is welcome to an occasional bottle of beer, and any driving that she has to do is given exclusively to him."

"Well, sir, I am sorry to have to say it, but it's a mighty poor business for a respectable man to have to engage in."

"Oh, indeed, I know it, but still I discovered something worse even than that the other night. A young fellow hired me not very long ago. He said: 'I want to look for a certain person on King street, so I'd like you to drive very slowly along the south side close to the sidewalk.' I said all right, and I did as I was told. Every once in a while he would say 'A little slower, cabby,' and I saw he was peering out of the window. By gob, says I, he is some American fly-cop after someone. But I didn't think that long. I heard him say something, and thinking he was speaking to me I leaned over and found he was talking to a young girl on the sidewalk. I heard her say: 'get out, you sneak.' I was on to him then. He just did it once more, when I jumps off the hack and told the girl to stop for a second, and I would see that the man who insulted her was punished. I hauled him out of the carriage and told him to pay me $3. He made a grand kick. 'All right,' I said, 'there will be a policeman by here in a minute.' That settled it. He paid me and escaped."

"That was a case where virtue was its own reward."

"Yes sir; three dollars for ten minutes' work. I was telling some of the boys on the stand about my adventure, and some of them were saying that there was a gentleman in the town here who used his private carriage for making mashes on young girls along the street after dark. A handsome carriage and a pair of horses is more than some girls can resist."

"What was the most exciting thing that ever happened you as a hackman?"

"Well now, that would be pretty hard to say. Oh, as a general thing there is nothing ever very special happens to a hackman. The time the block-paving was going on on King and Queen streets, last summer, I had a funny experience. I was on the York street stand one night when a young man with a black beard came up to me. There was a young woman with him, not very good-looking but pretty nicely dressed. He asked for a certain hackman. Well, we don't care, as a rule, about putting fares out of our own paw into that of any other driver. But this fellow happened to be next hack to me, and heard his name. Anyway, they got in, and I heard the man say, 'Drive me to the Humber.' Jim's going away left me first hack on the stand. I thought no more about it, but in a few minutes a real pretty woman came up to me and described this man, and asked me if I had seen him. I told her he had gone into a hack with a lady. You ought just to have seen that woman's eyes when I told her that. 'If you can catch—no, I think she said overtake—overtake that hack, said she, I'll give you $5.' Well, now, I knew they had gone to the Humber, and I was pretty sure they wouldn't drive very fast, so I bundled her in and got on the box. I wasn't very sure how far they had got with the block-paving on Queen street, but I wanted to strike what was fit to drive on as soon as possible, so as to make sure I wouldn't pass the hack. So I went along Richmond street to Esther and when I got there I found the street full of blocks. This kept me back, and we didn't catch that darned hack until we were on the lake shore road. When we got even with it I said, 'Jimmy, stop your load, I want to speak to you a minute.' He stopped, and when I assisted my fare out she was trembling like a leaf. She just went over to the other hack and looked in. I just saw her reach in her two hands and when she took 'em out she held in them the other woman's hat and feathers. She threw that on the ground and trampled on them and then reached for the other girl again. She fairly skull-dragged her out of the hack. I believe she would have choked her if I and another cabman hadn't pulled her away. And do you know, that big chump in the hack never interfered or said a word. He had a black beard and mustache, and his face was as white as a sheet. As soon as we pulled her away she just sat down in the sand and commenced to cry as if her heart would break. Then the man came out of the hack and came up to her: 'For heaven's sake, Kate, don't make an exhibition of yourself,' he said. Well, sir, women are the darnedest fools you ever saw. If she had gone to work and scratched the nose off her husband I'd never have interfered, but instead of that she tackles the woman, and when that mean villain began to talk to her and raised her up out of the sand she quieted down and drove off with him in Jim's hack. Oh women are queer ones. I'll bet that she puts all the blame on the other woman, and thought her husband was a perfect angel, who had been led astray by a designin' woman—that's what they call it. Well, I drove the girlie back to town, and when she had time to think she was hopping mad. Every time she'd look at her mashed hat she wanted to go and find that woman. She said she had as much right to him as the other woman, because he paid attentions to her before he was married, and only married the other woman because she was better fixed than she was. 'Yes, and better looking,' I said to myself. But the strangest thing that happened that night was that I was so flustrated that I let that woman go off without ever asking for my $5. But it was all right. A boy came up to me on the stand next day and handed me an envelope with a $10 bill and a slip of paper inside with writing on it, 'Fare to Humber and back.'"

CHAPTER IV.
BILLIARDISTIC BOYS.

There is no amusement I can think of out of which innocent enjoyment cannot be extracted. Personally, I can see no harm in young people dancing or playing billiards or cards—as long as they are carried on in the homes of these young people. As soon as our youth desire to pursue these pleasures away from the watchful eye of their parents, so soon do they become dangerous. The billiard halls of this city are not supported by men, but by lads. Go to any of them, either day or night, and ten to one you will find the majority of the players are youths not yet come of age. A remarkably large proportion you will find to be mere boys, and the skill with which they play seems to argue that they did not start playing yesterday nor the day before. Just watch the swagger they assume. The blase airs of these young cynics is an article of first-class quality. After you have admired that, I call your attention to the cut of the garments of these young gentlemen—very neat isn't it—and two or three of them sport watches, gold or silver. Then consider that it costs these cute-looking chaps 30 cents an hour for every hour that they occupy that table and that some of them are here every night, and you will wonder where the wherewithal comes from. Some of them work. Some of them don't. In any case they must have indulgent parents, or—something. There is a group of Upper Canada College boys round that table. No doubt their wealthy and aristocratic progenitors make liberal allowances to their darling boys. They play good enough to make a good showing in a tournament. If they are as proficient regarding the angles at the base and on the other side of the base of an isosceles triangle as they are with the angles in and about this table they must be fine mathematicians. There is another group playing pool. Don't look at them too hard, because they are chipping in ten cents on the game. One little boy who has not been playing very long, and who I saw scoop in a "pot" shortly after I came up stairs, has lost the joyous look that then mantled his features. Just study that face. Look at the dreadfully anxious expression with which he follows the movements of the ball, and as it creeps slowly towards a pocket I believe the intensity of that boy's will makes the inert ivory move an inch further on, and it drops in the pocket. He flushes up to the roots of his hair. If he gets the next ball he will take in the "pot" again. But he is very nervous, and makes a poor shot, and the next in hand pockets the ball. The little chap looks wistfully at the bigger boy who took in the forty cents, and goes up and whispers something to him. "I can't do it Charley. You'd only lose again. You've got no show with us, and you'd better get out of it while you can." Charley goes and sits down, feeling very bitterly I've no doubt. There is the spirit of gaming in its essential characteristic—after all of your own money is gone, borrow from anybody and everybody, and have another hazard.

I went up to another prominent hall in the daytime, and found it filled with youths, but they did not seem such a respectable-looking lot as those I saw at night at the first place. They were a hoodlum lot, very noisy, and poor players. I was much surprised. It seemed astonishing that during the working hours there could be such a number of young men unemployed and yet playing a game which it requires funds to engage in. There is something very ominous about this and no one could think otherwise than that times must be very flush indeed to permit of it.

A visit to a hall which is attached to a saloon showed me that this class of place is patronized mainly by men, nor was there half as much noise as in the room last mentioned. I am told that in some of these places they merely play for the drinks, and much drunkenness is the result.

Pool is at present the most popular form of billiards among the masses. It lends itself more readily to gambling than carom billiards, and any person who takes observation will come to the conclusion that more of the spirit of gaming is disseminated among our young men by this game than by any other half-a-dozen things. It would seem to be quite as necessary that boys should be prevented playing at all in public billiard halls, as it is that they should be prevented buying liquor at a bar.

CHAPTER V.
THE GAMBLERS.

The life of a professional gambler is not passed in a constant whirl of excitement, as the uninitiated may suppose; neither is it a continual source of pleasure to him, as many of the fraternity in Toronto could testify did they wish to relate their Police Court reminiscences, or the enjoyment they experienced during their somewhat erratic periods of "financial depression." The crime of gambling at cards increases with the growth of every city and for some reason or other the police make but spasmodic efforts to suppress it. This appears to be especially the case in Toronto, where the members of this thieving profession openly defy the detectives and laugh at the puny efforts of the police constables and their officers, who have sometimes occasion to visit the houses in search of thieves. Neither the constables nor the detectives are to blame for this deplorable state of affairs, but the heads of the department are, because they know that the evil exists; know that young men are nightly receiving their first lessons in those dishonest practices that tend to damn their whole future prospects, and yet will not issue the mandate that would rid the city of these unprincipled professional gamblers, these miserable curs of society. Not long ago, at a Police Court trial, the Magistrate remarked that he looked upon a professional gambler as a more degraded being than a common street thief, and explained his meaning by adding that a thief boldly takes the chances of securing his spoil or a term in prison, while the gambler first secures the confidence of his victim, and then by subtle cheating robs him of his money. And yet as a Police Commissioner he details about two hundred constables and seven detectives to hunt down the thieves, and allows the gambling hells to flourish on the principal streets. The Magistrate is not alone in this neglect of duty. Mayor Boswell is chairman of the Board of Police Commissioners, and his Honor Judge Boyd sits by his side. Are these gentlemen aware that night after night scores of young men are being

ENTICED INTO THESE DENS?

Are they aware that night after night they are exposing the children of their old friends, perhaps their own boys, to the temptations provided by the proprietors of these soul-destroying caves of iniquity,—to the fascinations of the gaming table? Are they aware that many young men highly connected in Toronto, have not only blasted their reputations and their prospects, but have rendered themselves liable to a felon's doom by robbing their employers to pay an "honorable" debt at cards,—a debt never really contracted excepting through the medium of marked cards or like devices? If they be not aware of these things let them study the police records, and should they not be successful in their search let them accompany a detective on night duty in his rambles through Toronto by Gas-light. The writer has done so on many occasions during the past ten years, and has witnessed such scenes of dissipation, such open cheating and deliberate robbery of inexperienced boys, and has heard so many expressions of remorse and despair that he cannot but feel surprised that the fathers and mothers who have wept tears of blood over their erring and deluded boys, that the merchants who have been robbed and the victims themselves do not rise up and demand the heads of the police department to suppress this gigantic evil at once. Perhaps they will when Major Draper, Chief of Police, gets tired of shooting alligators in Florida.

CHAPTER VI.
PLUCKING THE SUCKERS.

There are so many different devices resorted to by the professional gambler in order to secure the money of his victim without showing that he has been cheating, that it is almost an impossibility to recall them all from memory, but a few may be noted. The game of faro was so thoroughly described in the recent Mathieson-Kleiser Police court case that it is only necessary to show by a single illustration how the uninitiated can be cheated under his very nose without the slightest danger of the dealer being detected. In playing a brace game the dealer procures a deck known as "strippers," which are made out of thin and elastic cards. The deck is first cut perfectly square, and then trimmed in such a manner as to resemble a wedge, being a trifle wider at one end than at the other, so trifling that no one out of the secret could notice it. It is then decided if the deck is to be arranged so as to play one end against the other; that is the ace, deuce, tray, king, queen, and jack against the four, five, six, ten, nine, eight. The first-named cards, with two of the sevens, are placed together, making one half of the deck; then the latter-named cards, with the other two sevens, which constitute the other half of the deck, are placed together, being still smooth and even on the edges. They are then divided equally, after which one half is turned round, and you have a deck of "strippers," which the dealer can manipulate so successfully that it is impossible for a better to win. The "capper," who plays in with the dealer, the screw box, sanding the cards, playing with fifty-three instead of fifty-two cards, and preparing the cards so that two can be drawn from the box at once, and still adhere to each other, at the will of the dealer, are a few of the difficulties a better has to overcome before he can win any money at faro.

The most popular game played in the city, however, is draw poker, and this game is not confined to the gambler's den or the club room.

IN A FRAUDULENT GAME

there are generally two or more confederates playing in with each other as the opportunity occurs so as to rob the strangers at the table. If the victim be very fresh the gambler simply "stacks" the cards, which is readily accomplished by placing them in a desired position while putting the hands that have been played in the pack. They also pass cards from one to the other to strengthen each other's hands, deal from the bottom where they have cards prepared, ring in cold decks—that is, a pack of cards all arranged to suit the gambler, and exactly similar in appearance to the ones in use—utilize the false cut, and make "strippers" out of, say, four aces and four tens, so that the gambler is always sure of a "full" hand or four of a kind; but the most ingenious method of fleecing a young player is by using "marked" cards. To all appearances the backs of these cards are covered simply by a fancy pattern, but the gambler can read them off as he deals as readily as if he were looking at their faces, so that he knows the other players' hands before the player himself can read them off. It requires but seventeen different marks to a pack, four marks to designate the suits, and thirteen to designate the cards in each suit. The mark will generally be found in the shape of a heart, diamond, spade, or club worked ingeniously into the scroll work, but some times an old hand at cheating will buy a pack with marks that require a "key" before they can be deciphered.

CHAPTER VII.
THE WORK OF THE "CAPPERS."

Standing at the entrance to a prominent hotel on King street one summer evening some years ago were two stylishly-dressed young men, each with nobby canes, which they twirled carelessly as they nonchalantly puffed away the smoke from their cheroots, gorgeous jewelry and moustaches waxed out to a point as fine as a needle. To the envious and hard-worked store clerk they appeared to be gentlemen in looks, thoughts, actions, and living. To the detective, who was watching them, they were known as miserable stool-pigeons, "cappers" for a notorious gambling hell, situated in rear of a King street building, on the lookout for victims. And it was these vile, heartless scoundrels that caused George Reynott's ruin. His father was a well-to-do merchant in a country town near Guelph who had sent George to the city to gain a metropolitan experience in a wholesale dry goods house, but it would have been better had George been satisfied to remain at home with his father in the town where he was such a favorite. He was barely twenty-four years of age, frank in manner and pleasing in address, with a temperament not suited to withstand the temptations of city life. He came to the city with a light heart, full of energy and with bright hopes for the future. Now he is a broken down gambler, inebriate and burglar, serving out a ten years' term in Joliet prison, while his aged father lies in a grave prepared for him by his son's follies and crimes. The writer knows not when the "cappers" first made George's acquaintance, but the detective states that he had seen the trio together several times in saloons and billiard parlors, where they occasionally played a five-cent game of "shell out." Gradually George became imbued with a desire to see more of the world, and his wily companions, knowing that his father kept him well supplied with money, gave impetus to this desire by relating surprising stories of midnight escapades, card parties and champagne suppers. When the poor deluded victim first commenced to handle the ivory chips is not known, but in a very short time he became one of the most constant visitors to the luxuriously furnished hell. His repeated requests for money alarmed his father, and his frequent absences from work annoyed his employers to such an extent that they finally wrote to the father. The letter had its effect. Mr. Reynott came to the city, and after a conversation with the wholesale firm consulted a detective, who explained just how far George had gone.

THE SCENE BETWEEN FATHER AND SON

was a painful one, but it ended happily, the latter having promised never to touch a card again. He meant at the time to keep his word, but in less than a month the "cappers" regained their old influence over him, and he became more fascinated than ever with gaming. When he was unable to get more money from his father he pawned his jewelry, until one night he took the second decided step in the downward path. There were five seated at a table, George among them, two being strangers, and the other two being regular "skins," when the writer entered the room, but they were so engrossed with their play that they paid no attention to the visitor. It was draw poker, twenty-five-cent ante and five dollars limit, and much to the surprise of at least one person in the room, George was away winner, having half a dozen stacks of chips in front of him, along with a roll of bills and a pile of silver. His face was deeply flushed, his eyes sparkled, and his whole frame quivered with the intense excitement that consumed him, but when the "luck" commenced to turn, and he saw his chips and bills gradually fading away, a ghastly pallor spread over his face, driving back the gambler's blood to his heart. The "skins" had been utilizing a pack of "markers," and in order to rob the strangers had first dealt George the winners, so as to more securely hide their villainy, and had then fleeced him at their leisure. When the unhappy young man found himself completely ruined, with his I.O.U. for $25 in the hands of one of the gamblers, he was filled with a great remorse, and wept like the child he really was. He felt that he must pay the debt of "honor" contracted over the poker table or be

DISGRACED AMONG HIS "FRIENDS."

And he did pay it, but at the expense of his honesty and his employers. He stole goods from the store, pawned them to pay his gambling debt, was found out, and would have been sent to jail but for the respect the employers had for the father. After this exploit the reckless young man went headlong to the devil. He became a frequenter of the lowest gambling dens in the city, practised "skin" games till he became as skilful as his old-time "cappers," and his passion for the card table became so strong that when he could find no other game he would take a hand at "nigger loo" with the most notorious colored gang in the city. By this time his stakes had dwindled down from a $10 bet to one cent ante and fifty cents limit. He needed the balance of his cash for whisky! Three months ago the writer saw George Reynott making his way with "kindly curves" to a gambling house on King street. Last week a dispatch announced that he had been sent to Joliette prison for ten years for burglary.

Such is the brief history, and a true one it is, of a young man who, but for those miserable scoundrels known as "cappers," might have become a respectable member of society. Nor is this a solitary case. The gambling hells are nightly visited by young men well connected and refined in manner, but they are unable to resist the fascination of a game at poker. They play, and play high. They are on small salaries; where do they get the money?

CHAPTER VIII.
NIGGER LOO.

There are gamblers and gamblers, but in the expressed opinion of his Worship they are all thieves. Some affect good manners, society, and clothes, wear genuine diamonds, and claim for themselves the credit of never taking part in a "crooked" transaction, either over the table or away from it. They do not even openly associate with their "cappers," but leave these sneaks to do the dirty work, paying them a small percentage of the winnings therefor. They follow the "circuit," attend all the race meetings on both sides of the line, and are looked upon with favor by sporting men. They are lavish in their expenditure and generous to a fault with each other on the street. But alas for their good impulses! Every generous thought fades away more completely than a misty dream when they face each other at the poker table, and when they succeed in roping in a wealthy "sucker," they become night-hawks indeed, and swoop down on their unsuspecting prey with a force and ferocity that cannot be resisted. All thieves? Aye, cruel, heartless thieves.

There are other gamblers who affect—nothing. Too strongly in love with whisky to have much money, they simply drift on and on until the drunkard's grave or a government prison affords them a harbor of refuge. And yet, even these poor whisky-soaked half-crazed wretches, who are not possessed of spirit enough to look an honest man in the face, are thieves. They cannot play poker in the "gentleman" gambler's den, so they repair to the house of a colored man and by their superior skill in manipulating the cards fleece their darker-skinned, but not blacker-hearted brethren, out of the few pieces of silver they succeed in earning during the day.

Yet it is hardly a step from the gambler's palace to the drunken crook's den, and when the visitor passes in his tour of inspection from one to the other no feeling of surprise comes over him. The same kind of people are in attendance, are playing poker, and if they have not pat hands lying on their laps it is because they keep them concealed in their vests or down the back of their necks. You know even a gambler is allowed to smooth his shirt-front or adjust his collar when he wishes. The same kind of people, with faces a little more bloated and blotched, perhaps, and the lines showing more clearly the unmistakable

SIGNS OF DISSIPATION

and debauchery, but the very same kind of people. There is no place in the world better adapted for the study of human nature than in the poker room. So the reader may accompany a detective and the writer to one of the most notorious "nigger dives" in the city. It is a queer-looking attic about the size of a large cupboard, and is illuminated in daylight by a four-pane window that commands a picturesque view of outhouses and filthy yards. It is one of those noisome chambers upon the very threshold of which a sensitive person will probably recoil in natural disgust. The paper on the wall, or what remains of it, is discolored and greasy, and the table, once a light oak, has been blackened by the action of time and dirt, the unbrushed sleeves of the gamesters, tobacco smoke, and beer stains. There were five people, two white men and three "coons," seated at the table when the visitors managed to overcome their first feeling of disgust, and enter the room. Phew! It was worse than executing a search-warrant in a York street junk-shop. They were playing poker, and paid no attention to the detective, when they found he was not followed by a posse of police.

"It's all right, Slick; only showing a friend of mine around a bit."

"Good enough, boss; thought as you'se gwine to pull de ranch. Make y'seff to hum."

That being impossible in so small and filthy a hole, the visitors squeezed themselves as near to the open window as possible, and watched the game. It was evident at a glance that the white men were proficients in the art of cheating, and that the "coons" knew they were exercising their arts, but

THE FASCINATION THAT LED THEM

to the table kept them still in their seats. The deals go on, and as piece after piece of silver crosses from the stakes of the blacks to the whites, the silence becomes still more ominous, and the glitter of three pairs of rolling black eyes becomes more dangerous. The first coon deals the cards and all pass out, the next taking up the pack with a like result. Coon No. 3 clumsily shuffles the pasteboards, but does his "stacking" so poorly that every one gets on to his racket, to use a gambler's phrase, and passes out. Now comes a jack-pot, where every one antes till the game is opened. The pack circulates three times, and no one will open it, although the onlookers see a pair of aces in one hand which disappear in a most mysterious manner. The expression on the faces of the whites differs widely. One is as cool as if he were engaged in a game of euchre for the drinks; the lips of the other twitch nervously, his face is as pale as the whisky blotches will allow it to be, and his eyes have a peculiar shifting motion, as if he apprehended danger. But look at the coons! Their wooly heads are pushed forward till their necks look as long as a plumber's bill, their protruding eyes are as stationary as a fascinated gamester at a faro table, and their great flat nostrils are dilated so as to almost engulph their mobile lips, from which no sounds are issued. The pot is a large one for such a small game, and when the imperturbable white leans over and calmly observes, "I'll open it for a dollar," there is a dead silence, followed by a sudden move on the part of the largest coon, who leaps to his feet, and with flaming eyes, yells,

"No you don't, honey; you squidged dose keerds."

Every man makes a grab at the pile in the center of the table, which is overturned with the lamp, and in the

EGYPTIAN DARKNESS

that ensues a general fight occurs. The writer cannot say who got hurt; he got his body out of danger by changing venue to the roof. When he returned the crowd were equally dividing the money and the imperturbable white was disgorging aces and kings from behind his neck and out of his vest and sleeves.

If it were possible to confine gambling at cards to the professional gamblers, there would be no cause for complaint, but as this is an impossibility, the Police Commissioners should take steps to protect young men who are first innocent victims and afterwards by their experience become villainous cheats. It is a well-known fact that poker is largely played in private houses and at some of the clubs, but with these cases the police are powerless to deal, and it is only public sentiment that will break them up. In some of the hotels, too, rooms are set apart for card-playing, but as the Magistrate has stated that, on a hotelkeeper being convicted of such an offence, he will annul the liquor license, it is safe to conclude that the business is not carried on on a very large scale. The Police Commissioners have it in their power to keep many young men from being decoyed headlong to destruction. Will they exert that power by arresting these "cappers" and unscrupulous night-hawks as vagrants, if they cannot catch them gambling, and give them a term of imprisonment without a fine after the first conviction?

In conclusion it may be remarked that gambling is not the only offence of the gambler against public morals. Many of them shun drink, and only indulge in occasional excesses in this direction, but all of them, without exception, are frequenters of immoral houses. When a gambler makes a haul his first impulse is to repair to the bagnio, where he finds creatures who will welcome him when he is flush. The debasing nature of gaming is shown in the one fact that the money won is largely spent in the indulgence of guilty pleasures.

CHAPTER IX.
THE NIGHT POLICEMAN.

"Come along Teraulay street," said a night policeman the other night to me, "you may as well go that way to the office as any other." It was after one o'clock in the morning, it was a starless night, our footsteps echoed strangely from the houses, millions of unseen spirits were opening with noiseless fingers the swelling buds of the horse-chestnuts over head, and, in short, the night policeman by my side wanted to chat and thus pass some of the time away. I was not slow in taking advantage of the humor he was in.

"I suppose you have some queer experiences patrolling through the ward at night," I put in as a starter.

"Indeed I have," he replied as he adjusted his cape over his shoulders, "yes indeed. You would hardly believe me if I told you some of them. See here, Kate," addressing a woman who was slinking past in the shadows, "You had best get under cover somewhere. If I see you again I'll run you in, mind that." The woman scuttled away in the darkness, and the policeman, catching step with me again, continued, "Yes, it's a queer life we lead out in the street at night, and it's queer things we hear and it's queer people we see. Why, it's not half an hour ago that I was seeing down that street yonder when I heard a woman's screams and cries of murder. I could hear the sound of vicious blows, and was not long in locating the house.

"The screams grew louder, and, drawing my baton, I made a rush against the door and burst it open. As I entered the little hall the light in a back room was put out. I struck a match, and going through lit a lamp on the table. Well, sir, it was

A QUEER SIGHT.

A woman was crouching on the floor in her nightdress. Her face was swollen and bleeding, and there was a cut on her head. Her white garment was spotted with blood, and she was groaning with pain. In the corner stood her husband, a big, ugly fellow half dressed.

"What are you killing your wife for, Bill?" says I, "You'll have to come with me."

"I never struck her," says he.

"Indeed that's true, sir," said the woman, "I fell down the cellar stairs in the dark."

"But I heard you yelling murder outside."

"Sir, you must have been mistaken, I never cried murder. Did I, Bill. 'Pon my word, sor, it was by falling down the stairs I got hurt."

"'Show me the stairs,' says I, and would you believe it, there isn't a cellar in the place, nor stairs neither!"

"Did you arrest him?"

"Naw! where would be the use? She would come up in the morning and swear a hole through a brick wall that he never put a hand on her, and where would I be?—I'd look like a fool, and I would be reprimanded for bringing a case like that into court. Yes, I left them there, and as I was goin' out, what do you think but the fellow followed me and threatened to have me before the commissioners for breaking in his door. There are lots of scenes like that, lots of 'em. Why I have heard the devil's own ruction going on in a house, and when I went in there they were all sitting among a lot of broken furniture, as mum as mice and ready to swear that they hadn't opened their mouths to speak for twenty-four hours."

"What about burglars?"

"I have had some queer experiences. Ha! ha! One moonlight night I was pacing on my beat, when I saw a dark figure leap over a fence that surrounded the handsome premises of a wealthy lawyer. I went to the fence and looked over, but it was dark on the terrace and I could see nothing. In a few minutes, however, I saw

THE DARK FIGURE OF A MAN

crawling stealthily along the veranda and enter through an open window, and in a few minutes a faint light shone out. Fortunately I could hear in the distance a footstep which I rightly judged was the policeman on the other beat. I went up a block, called him, and the two of us returned to the scene of operations. After consultation I put my comrade to watch the window while I went round the house. I found a room on the ground floor dimly lit. I tapped on the window and in almost a moment I heard a man get out of bed and come to the window. It was the man of the house. He recognized me at once. I whispered to him that I had seen a man climbing through one of his up-stair windows. He never said a word, but beckoned me round to the front of the house and let me in. I told him what part of the house it was in, and we went softly up stairs. We could hear no noise nor did we meet anyone. We went in softly through a long corridor, and descending three steps entered what I took to be the servants' quarters. Suddenly my companion touched me on the arm and pointed to a strip of light under a door. We both came closer, and could hear a whispering inside. I asked him if I would burst the door, and he nodded. I drew back as far as I could, and then launched myself with all my force against the door, which gave way easily, and we both sprang into the room."

"Did you catch the burglar?" I inquired, as the policeman started to wipe his lips and look up at the sky.

"You bet we did. He was easy caught. In fact, he and the housemaid were—well, this is a queer world.

SUCH A SCENE

I never saw. The girl wept, implored, prayed and finally went into a fit. The "burglar" got down on his knees and begged for mercy, and the lawyer stormed and swore and finally laughed. The whole house was roused, and some of the women came in and cared for the wretched girl."

"Did you arrest the fellow?"

"No, the lawyer was satisfied with kicking the fellow into the street, and bundling the girl after him on the next morning, and that was the whole of it. It turned out that he had been in the habit of visiting her in this way for months, and he would not have been caught that time had it not been for the bright moonlight. He might have known better, but when a fellow makes up his mind to see his girl he will undergo any risk no matter what it is. I often meet him, and he looks mighty sheepish, I can tell you. See that high door-step?"

"Which, this one?" "Yes."

"Well, one frightfully cold night last winter I sat down on that door-step a moment to make an entry in my book. I had hardly seated myself when

I THOUGHT I HEARD BREATHING.

I was puzzled for a moment, and looked all around, but couldn't make out where the sound came from. Finally I decided it was under the door-step. I got down, reached under and pulled out two little children, a boy and a girl, half naked and nearly frozen. I took them to the station, where we thawed them out and saved their lives. They had been put out half-dressed by their drunken step-father, the poor little things had crept under the door-step for shelter, and if I had not found them when I did they would have been frozen to death as sure as fate. See that lane?"

"Yes."

"Caught a burglar in there in great shape. I was coming along very quietly one night when I ran against a fellow coming out of the lane. He made some excuse and hurried away as quick as he could, and after he got some distance he gave a loud and peculiar whistle. I felt that something was wrong, and went down the lane a little piece to where there was a high board fence. Some one called out, 'Are you there Flight?' I answered 'yes,' and then he said 'look out and catch,' and the next moment he threw a bundle of stuff over the fence, and it fell right into my arms. He threw over another bundle, and then he climbed over himself, when I collared him. He was the most surprised burglar you ever saw. I took both him and the bundles to the station, and he got two years. I never found out who the other fellow was, but he was no good anyhow, or he would have risked himself to warn his mate in some fashion.

"Yes," said the policeman, as he went softly up a couple of steps, tried a door, and then resumed his walk. "We have some mighty unpleasant experiences. 'Pulling a house,' as they call it, is not to my taste, but we've got to do it, all the same. We never know anything about it till we are paraded at twelve o'clock and marched away in a body. The house to be raided is then surrounded, men being placed in the rear and at all points of exit, the rest accompanying the sergeant into the house. Sometimes there is a great hullabaloo, but generally they keep mighty quiet. The last house I helped to raid was on — street. It was a mighty cold night, and they had no suspicion of what was going to happen. The house was pretty full and so were the inmates, and they were dancing and raising particular Cain. When the sergeant rang the bell they didn't stop, but after the woman of the house had peeped out and seen the police she gave one yell, and that settled it. We pushed in, and could see them dashing up stairs and flying for the rear of the house on all sides. One young fellow took it quite philosophically, lighting a fresh cigar and awaiting further developments. Those who ran out the back way were netted easily, and were brought back looking mighty crestfallen. None of the girls tried the escape dodge—they simply broke for their rooms to secure their valuables. Two who had never been arrested before set up a most lugubrious howling. They threw themselves down on the floor, tore their hair, and cut up bad. Another girl swore a steady stream of oaths for half an hour, while the rest cut jokes with us to cover their chagrin. The sergeant found one man under the bed. He hauled him out by the heels, and the expression on that fellow's face when the sergeant yanked him to his feet by the collar, would make a dog laugh. Another fellow had been hid his girl in a narrow closet, and when found he was bleeding at the nose. In a little while he would have been smothered. It was rather a queer procession back to the station. Some of them were singing, others crying, while the rest of them were swearing like dock-wollopers."

A CUTE GIRL.

"One morning about two o'clock I was pacing my beat in a neighborhood where a large number of wealthy people resided. All at once I saw a female figure coming swiftly towards me, and when she reached me she proved to be a young and very handsome girl. She was all out of breath and greatly excited. She could hardly speak for a moment, and then she gasped out that some one had broken into her house and was raising a disturbance. 'He threatened to kill me, sir; come along and arrest him.' I never hesitated to go with the woman, and I started off. She took me away three or four blocks, and brought me into a house where a dim light was burning. There were a few dishes smashed on the floor, and some of the furniture was overturned, but that was all. We searched the house and the premises, but could find nobody, and after wasting about an hour I returned to my beat. Would you believe it? Two of them houses had been burglarized during my absence, and over $3,000 worth of stuff carried off."

"And the woman—?"

"The woman steered me away from the spot while they went for the swag—you bet I'm not fooled like that again."

"Did you have her arrested?"

"Pooh! what good would that do, man? She would have stuck to her story, and that would settle it. There would be simply a suspicion that her little yarn to me that night was made up, but no jury or magistrate would convict her."

THE FINDERS.

"Hullo!" said my policeman friend as he glanced across at a house where a light suddenly appeared in one of the windows, "the finders are getting up."

"Finders; what are finders?" I inquired.

"It's no wonder you ask the question. It's astonishing the different ways that some people do make their living in this city. A finder is a man who makes his living by finding things."

"Go on."

"The finders are chiefly colored people, living in the Ward. They sally out just at daybreak, and dividing up into squads, slowly patrol Yonge, King and Queen streets on both sides. As they stroll along they carefully scrutinize the sidewalks, alley entrances, door ways and the gutter in search of lost articles, money, etc."

"I wouldn't think they would make much at that kind of work?"

"Yes, but they do. You have no idea of the amount of things lost on these streets at night. A drunken man may sprawl into the gutter and lose his watch, purse or some other valuable. He gathers himself up and goes on. In the dark the article is not noticed, but the first break of dawn reveals it to the professional finder. A drunken man may stumble into an alley and lose his hat, the professional finder gets it at daylight. Thieves arrested on the streets often stealthily throw valuables they have stolen into the gutter, and there they are sure to become the prey of the finder. A thief being pursued will throw away his revolver that would tell against him and the finder gets it in the morning. Oh, I tell you they sometimes come home with quite a boodle, and no one can say but they get it honest enough.

"Strange things occur on the streets, and some robberies have their funny side. One night a couple of crooks met a lawyer from a country town not a thousand miles from Toronto, very drunk in Osgoode lane. He was sitting down on a heap of stones, and wasn't able to get on his feet. He implored them to take him where he could sleep. They took him up the lane a piece and then told him that he was in their room, and that he was to undress and get into bed. He with many protestations of gratitude prepared himself for rest, and his two friends bidding him good-night, and hoping that he would sleep well, and further promising to call him early, walked off with his hat, clothes, and boots, which were found in a pawn-shop next morning, where they had got $2 on them. The stranger wandered around till a good-natured laborer going early to work discovered him and took him into his house. The lawyer repaid him well for it afterwards. I know the fellows who did the deed, but they were never arrested, as the lawyer did not wish it, and by the way he has never drank a drop of liquor since."

CHAPTER X.
THE SERVANT GIRL'S "FELLER"

The millionaire and the shivering beggar at his gates may differ in every other respect, but they have one feeling in common. Both desire to live, and to live one must eat. The most important concern of mankind, then, is to get something to eat. It is open to all to secure this desideratum by labor of one kind or another. Men choose different avocations to this end. One goes down in a drain at 7 o'clock in the morning and throws dirt till six at night, and gets a dollar and a quarter for it. Another creeps down to a store in the dark and silent hours of the morning, and by the aid of a jimmey and a bit and brace secures a sum varying in amount from a few dollars up to several thousands. These are representatives of two great classes in the community—the toilers of the day and the prowlers of the night. There are all degrees of prosperity in the ranks of the former and all depths of vileness and degradation in those of the latter. During the day they are distinctly apart. The banker, the lawyer, and the shop-man pass the gambler and the procuress on the streets and know them not. But when night assumes his dim dominion over the world smug respectability may be seen watching with bated breath

THE RATTLING OF THE DICE

upon the table or dallying with sin in the by-ways of the city.

Thus they sometimes mingle, surreptitiously and fearfully.

The night hawks! They are to be found in every great city. They are the excrescences of civilization. In cities of great population they are a constant menace to the public peace. Toronto is, perhaps, no worse or no better in this respect than other cities of equal population. That we have a sufficient number of these birds of darkness the police assert, and the newspaper man, whose duties take him occasionally to their haunts, knows. They are a strange race with a terrible philosophy.

"Why don't you brace up?" was asked of a young man who looked pretty miserable in the early morning. He was evidently suffering from the effects of his last night's orgies.

"I wish somebody would give me a chance to brace up," was the answer given, with a weary smile. "I know a nice bar where we could both brace up."

"Well, now, joking aside, you know your present life is killing you. You are still a young man; you have a good trade. Why don't you get to work and avoid all this trouble. Compare yourself with that young fellow on the other side of the street with his dinner can. His eye is clear; his tongue is clean and his lips are moist. Are yours?"

"That's very well put, but that story has got two sides. I'm feelin' a little tough now; but by noon I wouldn't change places with Vanderbilt. Ten minutes after I get my first rye I'll be in as good shape as the coon with the dinner-pail; then he'll have to sweat and work all day while I lay off beside a cool keg of lager or other choice stimilants. You can't preach to me about

THE ADVANTAGES OF HONEST LABOR.

I have tried it. You work nine hours a day and get spoken to like a dog. For this you get three meals a day and a bunk to sleep in at night. Your first meal you haven't time to eat, the second is cold and tastes of the tin pail in which it is carried, and the third is a mess made up of what was left by your boardin'-house missus and her youngsters at their last meal. I tell you I may not get my meals reg'lar, but they're daisies when I do."

It was hard to decide what to say to talk like this. It was suggested, however, that in one plan of existence there was a prospect of long life and the respect of your fellowmen; in the other there was simply death and disgrace.

"Respect be d—d. The kind of respect a man gets who has no money is not worth much. If I cracked a bank safe, and snaked a million dollars out of it, I'd get all the respect from my neighbors that any man gets. As for long life, I wouldn't want to live long if I had to work 60 hours a week for the pleasure of eating three poor meals a day."

This, or something similar, is the philosophy of the hawks. It is summed up in the phrase "a short life and a merry one." It is a rule of life which makes a man, presumably civilized, more dangerous than a savage. He has the instincts of the savage combined with more knowledge and power for evil. It is a philosophy which every right-thinking man should do his little all to combat. It aims at the foundations of society, and if its falsity could be made apparent in words of fire, the human family would be a gainer thereby.

It is surely not making too bold an assertion to say that the most hardened enemy of society was

ONCE A GUILELESS CHILD.

He or she must have at some particular time taken his or her first step on the road to infamy. Some particular form of allurement must have caught the youthful eye and dazzled the foolish brain. What are these allurements? Can our youth be made to recognize them and see whereunto they lead? We think they can. It would be well to show that the roses of sin bear fearful thorns, that the fruits of mere worldly pleasure turn to bitter ashes on the lips. The series of articles which are being published in these columns have this end in view. By showing how the vicious live we expect to show that the person who chooses to tread the way of vice will find it broad enough in all conscience with a-plenty of wayfarers in it, but he will also find that the thorns and cruel stones increase with each mile, until its final pages are trodden with bleeding feet and washed with unavailing tears. It can be shown, we think, that all the vicious classes simmer down at last to the same shuffling, shambling level. The young gambler, his tailor's pride, degenerates into the sniveling aged tramp, who in fluttering rags begs for a crust of bread at the poorhouse door, or else his elegant limbs wear penitential uniform behind the prison bars. The descent of the wicked woman is still more awful, still more shocking.

In these sketches our readers may hope, not for cooked reports to support any particular view of life and its relations, but for actual facts witnessed by our own staff, or else the views of people having knowledge or experience of the things whereof they speak. It is better in these things to speak so plainly that everybody may see where the disease lies, and thereby form a better idea of how a remedy may be applied.

CHAPTER XI.
ALL NIGHT IN THE CELLS.

The numerous police stations of the city, and especially the Central station are on account of the news and incidents which surround them, favorite fishing grounds for the reporters. There is scarcely an hour of the day or night, that a reporter alert, watchful and ever ready for business, may not be found in the Central station ready to pick up the slightest item of news and bear it in all haste to the paper he represents. The reporters know the working of each station almost as well as the officer on duty. I was standing one night on the corner of Jordan and King streets when I observed four young men coming from the direction of Bay street. They were all more or less intoxicated, but one of them, a young man whom I knew well and who I was aware seldom touched liquor was the drunkest of the lot. He was quarrelsome and very noisy, and it was not long before I saw the dark figures of two policemen crossing from the corner of King and Yonge towards the group. One of them expostulated with the young man, but he became indignant, then abusive, and was finally arrested and taken to No. 1 station. I followed the party, and when we entered the inspector's office I could see by the bewildered look in the unfortunate young man's eyes that he had never been there before. He was led to the railing round the inspector's desk, and that officer studied him coolly for a moment through the little wicket, and then demanded his name. The young man gave it mechanically, and in the same way told the place of his birth, his age, religion and employment. Then the orderly on duty went through his pockets, took from him his knife, watch and chain, money, papers, pipe and tobacco, and other articles, and then with a gruff "Come on, here," led him down. His arrest, his march through the gaping crowd in the brightly lit streets, his search upstairs, the subdued remarks of the police on duty, and the bitter clang of the iron door behind him had evidently sobered him. His heart is like water in him, and he feels his blood course chilly in his veins as he stands aghast, gazing about him in the strange place. The concrete floor, the row of iron doors, and oh, horror! worse than all, the battered old drunk, who comes reeling towards him with a "Hello, old feller, you in too? Shake!" fills him with a convulsive dread, a nameless terror that sets the cold sweat oozing from every pore in his clammy skin.

He shrinks from the repugnant old drunk with a shiver of loathing and flings himself down on a bench in a paroxysm of bitter tears. Yes, weep poor wretch! Down on your knees—down on your knees in this foul place and float your prayers to heaven. You are a young man yet, yours may not be unavailing tears, the best years of your life are before you—down on your knees!

The old drunk comes stumbling forward. "Wash yer cryin' for? Brash up, brash up—it's all in a life time, look at me." Yes, look at him! He's a dandy! His face is gray with drink, there are blood lines in the yellowish white of his dim, dry eyes, his beard and hair unkempt, his clothes muddy and tattered, and his shoes all broken. But the miserable old creature means well with the youth. "Brash up I shay, the world owes ush a living, an' we're goin' through the world for the lash time."

Going through the world for the last time! Ah!

The young man leaps to his feet with a fresh sensation of horror. What means that sound of struggling on the stairway—those fearful curses and frenzied cries of helpless rage that make his muscles quiver? The officers are dragging a fresh victim to the cells. He struggles with his captors every inch of the way. The door is flung violently open, and the wretch is thrown into the room. Is this a man or a lower species of beast? Its face is covered with blood, its matted hair stands stiff about its head, its eyes flash fire, and its covering is in tatters. The police drag it to a cell, shut it in, lock it up, and then, flushed and panting, stand looking in at it with an expression on their faces that we might expect to see on that of a hunter who had meshed a lion. Yes, it is a man—no other animal can curse. He springs to his feet with a hoarse roar, and taking the bars in his hands, shakes the gate with the strength of a maniac. He paces up and down his narrow cell, uttering wild cries of vengeance, till at last he falls upon his bench exhausted, and his labored breathing tells that he is asleep. More drunks! all noisy, all battered. One of them wants to embrace the young man, who springs from him with a cry of downright fear. Then the affectionate drunk becomes indifferent and wants to thump him, but, fortunately, he is too drunk to carry it out. The door opens, and a man comes in quietly this time. His hat is pulled down over his evil eyes and as he slinks to a corner "common thief" is marked on every inch of him. The affectionate drunk wants to embrace him also, but the thief rises with a growl and threatens to hit him a crack on the nose if he doesn't go and lie down and give him a rest. The door opens again, and a fashionably-dressed gambler comes in, whose last word to the officer at the door is to "Send for Tommy; he'll bail me out." The affectionate drunk stands in awe of the newcomer's good clothes, and the thief, with a side glance at his stylish pin, shrugs his shoulders, pulls his slouch hat further down over his eyes, and settles himself for a sleep. The gambler goes into an open cell and lies down, but I the young man paces the room with clenched hands and fevered heart. And so the weary night wears on, and as the gray morning touches the windows with its cool fingers one by one the drunks rouse themselves from their sleep and shuffle over to the water tap to quench the burning thirst that consumes their throats. Even these wretches can joke in their misery.

"That was a surprise party to your stomach, I bet," says one, as he watches another take his first eager gulp of water, which fairly turns to steam as it goes hissing down his fevered throat.

"Wouldn't a big John Collins go good now, eh?"

"Or a brandy and soda, yum, yum!"

"Water's a good thing to wash with," says another boozer, as he lays down the cup and shakes his head, "but it's no good to drink, not much."

Then they get sympathetic and friendly.

"What do you expect to get?" says one.

"Oh, sixty days this crack, nothing less."

"Been up before?"

"Have I? Humph! The old man'll spot me as soon as I get into the bull-pen."

"What kind ov a police magistrate have yez in this blasted town?" asks a boozer from the bench.

They all look at him admiringly, enviously.

"Never up before?"

"Never struck the darn town in my life till last night, and betcher life I'll git outen it, too, as soon as I git out o' jail."

"You'll git off on yer fust offence," chorus the rest, and they look upon him as a company of paupers would look on one of their number who had been left a legacy. By this time the sun fills the streets, the tide of life roars past, and the group of wretches await the peal in St. James' steeple announcing a quarter to ten.

CHAPTER XII.
THE POLICE COURT.

My experience as a police court reporter is considerable, and in this sketch I propose to give the readers of THE NEWS a sketch of the Magistrate's morning levee, in which those of the night who hawks come to grief during the hours of darkness appear to explain their shortcomings.

In the first place a description of the surroundings of the Police Court might, and doubtless will, be of interest to those who have neither the opportunity nor the inclination to visit the place and inspect it for themselves. The court room is not unlike court rooms all over the world. There is the raised dais for the presiding magistrate, there is the little pen in front and immediately below it for the clerk of the court. There is the table in front of that for the lawyers, the table for the reporters, the prisoners' dock facing the magistrate, and the railing through the center of the room to keep back the great unwashed. To the right of and below the magistrate, behind a little screened desk, sits the deputy-chief or the inspector on duty, with the prisoners' docket before him. And that is about all. The court opens with the regularity of clock-work at ten a.m. precisely, but the doors are unlocked at about half-past nine. Shortly afterwards

THE REGULAR HABITUES

of the court begin to arrive. People slip in by degrees and take their seats in that portion of the room reserved for the public. Here comes a poor, pale-faced woman, meanly clad and sick-looking, who with her thin, trembling hand vainly tries to conceal the mark over her eye dealt by her husband's brutal fist. She has come to appear against him. There, as she sits nursing her griefs and wrongs, she unconsciously falls into that swaying motion peculiar to a woman who is nursing her child to sleep. Here comes a middle-aged man, whose hairs are already white, and whose face is seamed with lines. The sorrow and shame that he feels does not obliterate the expression of stern justice on his face. He has come to see what can be done for his rascal of a son who is charged with burglary. He would not have come of his own accord, he would have let justice take its course, but the cries and moanings of the nearly-crazed wife and mother, whom he has left at home, has driven him here. He has come for her poor sake. Here comes a plainly dressed and modest looking girl, who is sueing for her wages that she earned in the mean kitchen of some meaner man. The quarter to ten rings out and as Micky Free's father would say "now the pop'lace" comes pouring in. They have been feasting their eyes on the Black Maria, which has just discharged its contents into the station below. They are white, speckled, saddle-colored and black. They are well and poorly dressed.

ALL OF THEM ARE UNSAVORY.

Meanwhile a more interesting class of habitues are fast arriving. The deputy chief walks in with a dignified mien with his docket under his arm, lays it on his little table, opens it, scrutinizes it, makes an alteration here and there, and then sits down. A few lawyers come through a side door in a great hurry, fling their bags down on the table, glance at the clock, look very much relieved, give the crowd behind the rail a sharp, shrewd glance which takes them in one and all, even to the gurgling baby in the arms of that woman with the wet red mouth and the big moist eye. The reporters come rushing in, glance over the docket, nod to the lawyers, whisper with a policeman, fling their paper on the table, borrow somebody's knife and set about industriously sharpening their pencils. A couple of sergeants from the other stations arrive and consult with the deputy-chief. Three or four detectives come in briskly and confer with them. Then an inspector and some more sergeants and police come in and, standing erect, look about them with solemn and dignified air. The deputy critically compares his watch with the clock. A couple of policemen are immediately on the alert. It is four minutes to ten.

"Bring in the first two prisoners!"

The alert policemen go out and in an incalculably short time bring in two drunks, who are planted in the dock and told to sit down.

Says the deputy, "Is that John Smith and Reuben Robertson?"

"Yes, sir."

"Which is John Smith?"

"The man on the other side."

"Very well."

Then there is an expectant lull. It is

EIGHT SECONDS TO TEN.

As soon as the last second is buried in the grave of time that side door will open and the Magistrate will come in. The bells in St. James' steeple go "kling, ling, ling"—there, didn't I tell you. The side door swings suddenly open and to sharp cries of "Order! Order!" a tall, handsome military man with iron gray hair and moustache and dressed chiefly in a frock coat, the tails of which are flying behind him, darts into the room and with three long dragoon-like strides is in his seat. He fires a little battery of nods all round and the deputy steps up to swear to the informations. Then he whispers with the deputy a moment and smiles. Then he leans over and whispers with the clerk and laughs noiselessly, then he clears his throat, surveys the court room with the eagle glance of a veteran reviewing a troop of hussars, and finally consults the docket before him. He looks up sharply at the two wretches standing in the dock and asks which is John Smith. John is terribly sober, red-eyed, and befrousled.

"John Smith, you are charged with being drunk on — street on the — of May. Were you drunk?"

"Yer 'anner, I was afther going down to —."

"Were you drunk!"

"—goin' down to McBoasts, pwhin who shud I—."

"Were you drunk!!"

"—phwin who shud I meet bud—"

"Were you drunk!!!"

"—bud ould Mullin's son, and sez he to me, John, sez he—."

"Were—you—drunk?"

"I was, faith."

"Why didn't you tell me that at once?"

"I was tellin' ye all the time, yer anner, bud—"

"Were you ever up before?"

"Och, ax me no kushtions—sure you know right well oi was."

"Fined $1 and costs or thirty days in jail. Reuben Robertson—is your name Reuben Robertson?"

"It is, sir."

"You are charged here with being drunk last night. Is that so?"

"It is not, sir."

"Who arrested this man?" queries the magistrate.

"I did, sir," says a policeman promptly. He steps into the witness stand, lifts his helmet, is sworn, drops his helmet on his head again, and faces the prisoner.

"Was this man drunk as charged?"

"He was, your Worship. He was so drunk that I had to get a handcart to bring him to the station in."

"Do you hear that?"

"Yes, sir."

"Were you ever here before?"

"No, sir, and if you'll let me off this time, I'll leave the city."

"Discharged!" and Reuben makes a bee-line for the door. The French adopted the hat at one time as

A TOKEN OF LIBERTY.

They were judges of human nature. The first impulse of a prisoner discharged in that police court is to clap on his cap. More drunks follow. The old, old story. One man is charged with being disorderly as well as drunk.

"He struck me and tore me coat," says the constable who arrested him.

"Yes," pipes up the inspector, "and in the station below he was very obstreperous."

"Fined $5 and costs or sixty days."

Then the wife-beater takes his place in the dock. A low-browed, bull-headed, thick-lipped ruffian with bloodshot eyes. He leans his arms on the rail and gazes round him with a sulky air. His wife creeps reluctantly into the witness box—she keeps her face averted; she cannot trust herself to look at her husband. He pleads not guilty. "She tripped on the rug and fell against the table, yer Worship."

"Is this true?"

"It is not, your Worship," says the poor woman. "He—he struck me with his fist," and here she breaks down and sobs hysterically.

"Do you hear what she says?" queries the magistrate.

"She's lyin to you, sir."

"I would rather believe her than you," says the Magistrate, "I fancy a term in jail—or, say Central prison, would do you good."

"Oh, don't send him to jail, sir," cries the poor woman; "don't send him to jail."

"But he will only beat you again."

"Yes, I know, sir; but then the children—the children; where could they get bread and him in the jail, sir?"

It is enough. The man in the dock winces like one who is stabbed. A thrill runs through the court. The man is discharged.

The youth accused of burglary is led in. He is sullen, defiant, but uneasy withal. The detectives are not ready to go on with his case, and he is remanded. The father makes an ineffectual appeal for bail, and then goes home—home, ah! This furnishes the criminal docket!

An abusive language case comes up. Mrs. Drake is charged by Mrs. Gosling with the offence. Mrs. Gosling is a sharp-featured lady in an old-fashioned bonnet and a tired shawl. Mrs. Drake is the woman with the wet lips, the moist eye and the baby.

"Now," queries the Magistrate good naturedly, "what is this all about."

"Your Worship," says Mrs. Drake, "she called me a dirty scut."

"Oh, listen till her! listen till her!" shrieks Mrs. Gosling, raising her hands and eyes, "how can you tell a lie like that and you on your oat?"

"What is a scut," queries the Magistrate.

"Oh, Your Worship, I wouldn't shame myself by using such a word."

"I never called her a scut!" screams Mrs. Gosling, "I never did. She sed I wasn't married to me man."

"Neither ye are."

"Oh, ye lyin' hussy, how dar you stand there and—"

"Come, come," says the Magistrate, and with the aid of the police both women are quieted down and after much trouble all the witnesses are heard and Mrs. Gosling is fined $1 and costs. Shortly after eleven, however, all the cases are disposed of, the crowd disappears, the reporters rush off to their offices and the room is locked up until the next day at ten.

CHAPTER XIII.
PROMENADING THE STREETS.

This is Yonge street at 10.30 on a Thursday night. I will take up my stand in the shadow of this corner and watch the crowds roll by. What a moving mass of young folks, for the overwhelming majority are young folks. Some of them too young. It is after ten, and yet this bunch of juveniles moving south are not going home, judging by what I observed while I was walking, for I have been as far north as Elm street. I wouldn't be surprised if those two very immature maidens in the kilted skirts passed up and down two or three times yet. I have some difficulty in recognizing them, for there are 100 girls on the street who appear to have been got up on the same model. There may be slight differences of dress not discernible by the average male eye, but in essentials this seems to be a distinctive class. For the most part the other loungers on the street take it easy—walk slowly and languidly, but this tribe of whom I speak are in couples, and they walk along with a fine, graceful, swinging gait that carries them swiftly forward. None of them are out of their teens. Their dress is not loud. The colors are subdued, and the style of the Kate Greenaway order. The skirt is short, and enables a curious on-looker to decide the color and

TEXTURE OF THE HOSE WORN

and the plumpness or attenuation of the young woman's ankles. They are certainly youthful, and this short skirt makes them absolutely girlish in appearance, but in other respects by bold and artistic padding they attain a robustness, not to say matronliness, which is rather paradoxical. The swiftness of their walk makes them really the most noticeable personages on all Yonge street.

Anyone who sees them oscillating regularly between King and Queen streets would come to the conclusion that they are on "the mash," but if you select a couple and keep them in sight for a little while you will find that they entirely ignore the presence of the men whom they encounter in their path. These latter, however, do not ignore the girls. They are frequently greeted as they go along with low-toned remarks, such as "Hello, girlie!" "Good evening, Birdie!" and with sounds which I have observed are produced when one person kisses another. To these endearing salutations they either vouchsafe no notice or else they treat the intruder to such a reply as causes him to let them pass unnoticed the next time. This class of our citizenesses seems to me to be a very modern production, and their habits and usages had cost me some thought.

"Why do they parade up and down the streets?" I said to a long-headed detective friend, who sometimes gives me pointers and cigars. "They don't seem to be

HERE TO MAKE 'STRIKES,'

and they are not shopping, and if they want to take the air it is neither necessary to walk so fast nor take to such a crowded street. I suppose it is none of my business, but, my dear fellow, I believe in the saying which the Greek dramatist puts into the mouth of one of his characters, 'I am a man, and whatever concerns men interests me.' Of course this concerns girls." Taking no notice of this brilliant sally, my friend went on to say: "You think these young women are not intent on making a strike. Those two we have just passed, and who took no notice of your wistful gaze, would have returned it with interest if you had been the proper sort of a party. Those young women, sir, are the best readers of human nature with whom I am acquainted. They took you in at a glance, and they said, 'He wouldn't stand the biled eysters or the Inja pale ale.' I know that pair of business-like females, but I do not know their exact capacity for bivalves and beer. I am certain though that it is phenomenal. Now, there goes another miss, some of whose history is familiar to me. She is pale-faced, with thin, straight nose and sphynx-like expression. That icy little thing black-mailed a prominent merchant of this town not long ago, and almost tortured him into his grave. Detectives were hardly able to scare her off. There is another who, if she prevailed on you to get into a cab with her, would try to make you believe that you were a very bad man, and it would require a portion of your salary, paid periodically, to

ALLAY HER RUFFLED FEELINGS.

"Where do they live?"

"Most of them live with their relatives. Some of them work by fits and starts. I assure you they are as passionless as marble statues, and yet they are as fully cognizant of the nature and constitution of man as the most learned professors of the universities. I believe that the great majority keep themselves personally free from gross immorality, yet in their pursuit of what they think to be fun, combined with pieces of cloth, silk hose, high-heeled boots and bright ribbons, they go as near the fires of sin as it is possible to go and not get scorched, though I can assure you that the smoke of evil has so blackened them that they are morally as bad as those who have fallen, and should be avoided by decent men and virtuous women."

"On what then, do they base their claims to man's gratitude. I mean that gratitude that expresses itself in presents of gewgaws and finery?"

"It is all built up on hope and fear. I tell you, sir, that these maidens—there's Polly B— just gone by; I'll tell you something about her presently. These maidens, as I was saying, find their chief game among the ranks of the old, staid, bald-headed married men. These old fellows in whom wickedness lives though youth be dead, are flattered by what they think to be a mash made on one in whom throbs

THE FRESH BLOOD or GIRLHOOD.

It is simply wonderful how easily such men—shrewd old fellows that could bargain with Shylock on the Rialto—can be hood-winked and hoodooed by a slip of a girl. But I could tell you of scores of cases where toothless old men have been led a terrible dance by just such a girl as that Jessie C., who this moment flitted by us."

"What is the end of all these goings on?"

"What is the end of it? The end of it is often very close to the beginning. A few weeks shows our old Romeo that Juliet may be young, but she is not innocent. In some cases they make an endeavor to stick to their victim, but as a general thing they soon get everything out of the old fool, and then laugh at and discard him."

"But I mean what becomes of the girls?"

"Well, sir, wonderful to say, in a great many instances they don't go from bad to worse, but sometimes improve. I know some of them who have got married. I can't say that any of them are happily married. In most cases the husbands must have known all about the "amusements" which occupied his wife's attention in girlhood, and are as lacking in decency as she ever was. Probably he was not only aware of it but shared in the "gifts" extracted from "his old nobs," as they affectionately name their victims. But wonderful as it may seem, some of these unions are blessed with considerable happiness."

"You say that many of them amend their ways. What about the others?"

"The others are to be found in the fast houses of Toronto, Hamilton, Detroit, and Buffalo."

"Well, don't you think that even that is a very dreadful state of affairs? The way you speak one would think that it was a subject of congratulation that

MORE DID NOT GO TO PERDITION."

"Perhaps I do speak a little more hopefully than the facts warrant, but it seems to me so remarkable that any of them should escape going completely to the bad that it perhaps gives that tone to my remarks."

"Have you ever formed any idea how such an evil as this might be lessened?"

"I have thought of it often. My opinion is that parents are largely responsible for it. There is no use in talking, a mother or father is very much to blame if they allow their children to be out on the streets till all hours without knowing what they are doing. I tell you, sir, one of the most serious signs of the times is the slackening of the authority of parents. Children now-a-days, except in rare instances, have not that reverence for their parents which was inculcate when I was a boy."

"There's a good deal in what you say, but don't you think that it is but the natural reaction from the manner that was formerly adopted by parents towards their children? Instead of respect and love, parents tried to inspire their children with fear and awe. There surely is a happy medium."

"There is; but only a wise and conscientious parent strikes it. I know of cases where children know almost any other man

BETTER THAN THEIR FATHER.

They see him but seldom, and wouldn't care if they saw him less. The mother is perhaps weak minded and characterless, and as a consequence the children are allowed to drift wherever their inclinations or their passions direct. Poverty is no reason why a father should neglect the training of his children. Indeed, the poor man has often more chance to keep an eye on his offspring than the rich man whose time is taken up with business and society. So that poverty is no excuse for this sad neglect. Just to illustrate what I mean: Two weeks ago I saw on the street a girl dressed very richly. She wore a silk dolman, trimmed with rich fur. Everything else was to match in costliness and richness. Four years ago she was a small girl whom I saw every day. She was as slatternly a little thing as you would see in a day's walk. But as time went on there came a change in this and she began to spruce up. The change was very rapid. Indeed, not only did she show more neatness of dress, but actually the articles she wore were of a value that would naturally cause anybody to enquire where did she get them. But natural as would seem such an enquiry her parents neglected to make it, and finally she threw off the mask by openly adopting a life of shame. Then her parents bewailed and moaned at their misfortunes. I was looking after some ostrich feathers which were stolen, and in the search for them I had occasion to visit a house of ill-fame on Albert street. In this house S— had taken up her abode. She knew me and knew that I was acquainted with her whole history. I questioned her and her answers were to the effect that she was quite satisfied with her life, and thought that it was infinitely to be preferred to that which she had led as a girl at her home. She is not naturally bad, but her training had been such as to make her believe that any way by which good clothes, nice food and some fun could be obtained with little work, was the way which it was best to take. She forgot or never comprehended her loathsome, beastly shame, and compared her slovenly, loveless childhood with her present condition of rich fare, fine feathers, lovers, race-meetings and theaters, and decided that the latter was the best. Poor girl—poor wretch, I might say—if she could only pierce the future and see the end of it all. She's on the hill-top of shame now, where the sun is shining, but God help her when she goes down, as surely she will, amongst the slime and dirt which she will find at the foot, and in nine cases out of ten it does not take over three or four years to go from the top to the bottom."

CHAPTER XIV.
AN ALL-NIGHT MEETING OF THE ARMY.

The crash of tamborines, the jarring roar of a badly strung snare-drum, and the troubled, fitful echoing of a discordant chorus breaks through the quiet atmosphere of the darkening street. People turn and look back, some with a look of perplexity, others with a smile of contempt, while those going in the direction of the sound quicken their footsteps. As they pass us we hear them say "the Salvation Army—an all-night meeting," and instinctively we turn and follow them. As we draw nearer the people on the sidewalks thicken, while the music, which in the distance sounded at first like the wild air of a street minstrel ditty, assumes the style of a religious chant. The music, if it can so be called, issues from a dark, dense circular mass of people in the middle of the street. Suddenly it breaks into nervous and excited motion, and takes up a line of march, led by a man who walks backwards, facing those who follow, and beating time with a baton. He leads them in a high pitched, cracked voice, which at the higher notes becomes positively painful, but is always earnest and impassioned. It is a motley group that follows him. Prominent among them are the women, who, regardless of the mud and slush, heedless of the coarse and impertinent remarks of loafers as they pass, trudge patiently, singing in a chirpy, squeaky voice, which has been utterly broken and toggled up by constant and strained use in the chilly, open air. Some of them are

YOUNG AND PRETTY,

slyly watching the crowds as they pass, while others of them are middle-aged and hard-featured, the material of which grass widows are made. Each of them carries a tambourine which they beat out of all unison, and which, did they but know it, are calculated to do more harm than good, as their music is enough to drive any man to madness. On they march, the wild, weird music rising an falling fitfully, while every now and then the sharp ejaculations of "Praise God!" "Hallelujah!" etc., cut through the clangor like nervous shafts of sound. On either side of the column march a mob of men, women and urchins, some jeering them, others sympathizing with them, while hundreds tramp along out of sheer curiosity. The crowd thickens, sways forward anxious to obtain favorable seats in the hall, as it is now known to all them that there is going to be a "knee drill and an all night hand to hand fight with the devil while the gates of hell are to be stormed towards morning by the forlorn hope." The long, low barrack-like building is reached, the wide doors are flung open and the eager mob follow the soldiers with a rush into the vast and garishly lit interior. Then a scene opens on the eye which can only be witnessed in a great city. The high amphitheatre at the far end is soon densely packed by Salvation army soldiers, both men and women, most of the former dressed in red and blue coats with the breast illuminated with medals in various designs. The huge barn-like edifice is filled as if by magic and by all classes of citizens, from the devout woman sitting patiently in front, who has come to listen and to pray, down to the brazen-faced night hawk in the jockey cap and bangs, who has come to see and be seen and to make a mash if she finds a victim. And how many of such are here! Their cold, calculating, treacherous eyes watching stealthily the crowds of

SMUG-FACED YOUTHS

that occupy the lower part of the hall. Still the crowd comes pouring in until the place is packed to the doors, and then for the first time a partial stillness falls upon the place. There is a slight commotion in the front row of the elevated stage and then amid a crash of tamborines and a roar of voices chanting a spirited chorus, a woman with a pale, spirituelle face and fine, intelligent eyes, shaded by a plain black straw bonnet bound with red ribbons, steps to the front, stands still as a statue, and looks with a strangely pitiful expression over the vast crowd before her. Even after the music ceases, she still stands there, with fingers tightly clasped and lips moving in silent prayer, and then, suddenly and unexpectedly, she flings herself down on her knees, her whole body shaken with spasmodic sobs. The great crowd is thoroughly stilled now. All eyes are bent upon her, some in alarm, some in pity, while others burn with the kindling fire of religious fervor. She rises slowly and, stretching out her trembling hands to the audience, cries in a clear, bugle-like voice, "Oh, why will you die?" and then overcome by her feelings, bursts into a torrent of tears again. A thrill runs through the vast assemblage, all have caught the infection from her, and even the brazen-faced female in the back seat lets fall her eyes with a guilty look. Once more the electric woman on the platform begins to speak—at first brokenly, and gathering strength as she goes on, bursts out in an appeal to sinners, in which the terrors of a real old-fashioned up and up fire and brimstone gehenna are painted with a vividness which would

DO CREDIT TO A TALMAGE

or an old-time backwoods hard-shell Baptist preacher. She talks with a rapidity that is marvellous, every fibre in her willowy body vibrates, her eyes shine and her thin hands beat the air and rend the countenance of an imaginary Satan. She continues to speak until completely exhausted, and when she ceases another mighty chorus fills the hall. One after another the soldiers get up and relate their experience. Yonder is a man who used to be a dry-haired and gray-faced drunkard; now he is a man with new life coursing in his veins and shining in his eyes. He tells what the Lord has done for him, and as he relates the story his wife, who will never be beautiful again, for twenty years of unceasing misery have stamped themselves upon her, falls upon her knees, and, with the fast tears flowing down her cheeks, cries, "Yes, it's all true, thank God, it's all true!" That girl who is speaking now used to be a night hawk herself, but no one can mistake her earnestness. And thus the night wears on amid the crash of discordant music and the wailings and cries of the converted. The crowd begins to thin towards twelve o'clock, young men and women meet at the door, exchange a glance and a whispered word, and then slide out into the darkness. Suddenly there is a tumult in the lower part of the hall. A cry of "fight!" a savage oath, the audience rise as if by magic, and two or three muscular soldiers wrench a disorderly visitor to the door and fling him into the street. The singers sing till they are hoarse, the talkers talk till their voices crack, the exhorters look wan and ghastly, the tamborine players fall asleep in their seats, the noisy place stills frequently, and by four o'clock in the morning the last of them steps through the entrance and finds his way through the grey streets towards home.

CHAPTER XV.
THE "SCHOOL."

Ask any old and experienced officer on the police force, What does more to corrupt the morals of the young men and young women of this city than anything else, and he will answer almost certainly, "These dancing schools." And if he added that they also did more to undermine the constitutions of many a "buirdly chiel and bonny lassie" than even the doctors do, he would also be right. You will hear a young man or woman talk about "going to school," but you do not need to be deceived into thinking that they are taking a course at the public night schools. The arts taught in the school that they attend, they are already probably very proficient in.

Some eight or nine years ago these dancing assemblies were very common, and were attended by nice people, but year by year they have grown worse until the average "school" of the present day would be shocking and ruinous to any girl of correct sensibilities.

The "school," and its congener the hop, or dancing social, is invariably held in some public hall. A committee is formed by a number of young men, who stand to make some money if the "school" is a popular one. The committee should be composed of fighting men, as there is a good deal of constabulary duty to be done. At most of the schools the fair sex are admitted free, and quite a number of the blushing damsels who cannot get a "fellah" take advantage of that rule. When they get into the hall, however, they run a fair chance of

PICKING UP A CAVALIER

who came to the festivities unattached. On one occasion a spectator who had made up his mind to pry into the mysteries of a school which met in an east end hall, near Queen street, was rummaging for his entrance fee when a buxom young lady came blithely forward and addressed the janitor in a tone of reproach, "You're not going to charge the reporder, are ye," and the change collector expressed himself to the effect that he never had any intention of charging such a distinguished personage. Mendacious youth!—he had his hand extended for the coin and a fixed expression on his face that meant to get it or die. I did not remember having ever been introduced to the lady before, but I was very grateful for her kindness and flattered that I was so widely known. Seeing that I was known it behooved me to retire to a corner far from those who knew me. I had not long been there, however, before another man in a shepherd tartan shirt and minus collar or tie came up and volunteered to give me any information concerning the ladies and gentlemen on the floor which I desired. Without being bid he went off into graphic biographical dissertations on these, but as they were of an exceedingly scandalous nature I would not promise him that they would be published. One lady, whom he designated Big Mouth Moll, and who must have rivalled Messalina in the variety of her amours if this young man were to be believed, he was especially severe upon.

"Will you put that in, reporter?" he said.

I explained that Miss B. M. Moll was undoubtedly a lady, and that it might wound her feelings to publish facts concerning her "little accidents." He went away very much disgusted with me.

A more intelligent "scholar" whom I met confirmed a good deal of my collarless friend's unfavorable account of

THE GENERAL MORAL TONE

of the assembly. He said he knew them all, and that they nearly all worked in different industrial establishments in the city, and that pleasure rather than lucre ruled their lives.

One young woman was calculated to attract attention in particular. Her face was colorless, with the exception of a slight flush that seemed to flicker over her sunken cheek. She was languid, and after each quick movement of the dance a quick little gasp escaped out of the faded rose of her lips. Everything betokened a life being extinguished by consumption's chill embrace. She was an object for tender solicitude, but the burly curly-headed young ruffian who dragged her through the dance seemed not to be aware that a grisly guest was following at his heels to claim his partner for another scene than this.

I gathered from a remark made by one of the ladies that something had been going on of which I had not been cognizant. She whispered that "O'Brien was as drunk as Billy Bedam," and investigation showed that quite a number, while not as drunk as the historical Mr. Bedam was in the habit of getting, were pretty well on. Having therefore seen enough to disgust me I left.

This perhaps is an unusually low type of the "school," but the best is only a degree or two higher.

Most of the persons present were boys and girls born and reared in this Canada of ours. I am confident from what I have observed that these young women will become the wives of these or similar young men, and it is pitiable and humiliating to think that another generation of Canadians will grow up under the tutelage of such parents. Free schools are a failure if they cannot teach a man that squirting tobacco juice over your dancing partner's shoulder is bad manners.

And yet parents permit their daughters to go to such places, and be dragged down to the level of the lowest, not only in actions and conversation, but in the habits of thought which such associations create.

CHAPTER XVI.
THE GENUS TRAMP.

"One half the world knows not how the other half lives," and for the matter of that doesn't care. The "one half," by which in all probability is meant the well-to-do portion of the community, neither know nor care how their impoverished "brothers and sisters" (dearly beloved of course) live, nor for the matter of that how they die. Reader, gentle, fair or otherwise, were you ever the unhappy possessor of that rather unnecessary article known as the "key of the street?" Have you been out visiting until the "wee sma' hours," and on returning to your lodgings found that you had left your latch-key at home, also your cash, and the dread of your irate landlady, to whom you probably are in arrears, prevents you from rousing the house up? You have no intimate friend to quarter yourself on, not sufficient money to pay for bed and breakfast at a first-class hotel (the only ones accessible at that hour)? If so, then you must per force make use of your key of the street, or, in other words, tramp the city the remainder of the night, or rather morning, until long after "Faint Aurora dawns."

If, gentle reader, you have gone through this, to you, trying ordeal, you will readily comprehend some of the situations that I will try to describe in this paper. If not, I will endeavor to enlighten you as to the ways and means used in struggling or rather shambling through the world by those enfants trouves, known to the benevolent as, "homeless poor."

I speak of their ways and means rather than manners and customs, which may be described as the midshipman wrote down in his journal, the "Manners and customs" of the Fiji Islanders: "Manners—None. Customs—Nasty."

How many of the 100,000 and odd (and some of them are very odd) people of Toronto, who in their daily walks abroad, come across at intervals numbers of squalid, unkempt, ragged, and

RUM-BLOSSOMED BEINGS,

ever give a thought as to how these miserables live. Where did they come from? Where are they going to? How do they get their food, and above all, where do they rest at night? Such questions as these never bother the brains of the gay gentlemen and ladies fair who when out for a walk meet these bedraggled wights. They see them and turn away in disgust. Even the ladies bountiful who (to their honor be it said) have their own pet charitable institutions, know them not; they also, like the priest and the Levite, pass them by. These objects that you meet, ladies and gentlemen, are mostly professional tramps, and a most uncanny tribe they are. A great many of them have seen better days, but misfortune, disappointments, blighted hopes, and above all an overwhelming craving for alcoholic stimulants, fostered in their palmy days, perhaps by champagne, Hockhiemer, and Moselle, but now only satisfied by the soul-corroding whiskey which they love, has brought them down to their present condition. Many of them, however, are born vagabonds, who have been "constitutionally tired" since their infancy. Some of them have trades, which they are too lazy to work at, even if their whisky-shattered nerves would allow them; but they are too far gone now to attempt anything in the shape of industry. Besides, what mechanic or tradesman would hire them? They are in rags and filthy, and an unholy and pungent atmosphere, suggestive of an ancient distillery, pervades their surroundings. These aromatic gentry, as I before stated, are tramps, proper, pure, and simple. The nomadic harbingers and epitomes of all that is squalid, wretched, and poverty-stricken in the land. Hopeless, hungry, and miserable, they tramp on their weary way, friendless, forgotten, and unknown until, upon the mattrass of some jail hospital, or out in the fields beneath the stars, they breathe their last and take their final tramp.

I have given you a picture of the ordinary tramp, who overruns the continent from Collingwood to Galveston, from Portland to San Francisco, and is merely an ill-omened bird of passage, as in contradistinction to our

LOCAL VAGABONDISTI,

who remain year in and year out in our midst; and it is of these miserables who have made Toronto their field of action, or rather inaction, that I wish particularly to speak. Go down, let us say, to the Market square, any day during the winter, or in the months of navigation to the Esplanade. Hovering around the doors of the omnipresent "saloon" they lounge, a motley crowd. Occasionally, if the weather is not too rainy or cold, they may be seen posing on the lee side of a corner house, smoking clay pipes of unknown age, or chewing black strap in meditative mood. But the grog shop is always their objective point, and they seldom go far from its beery borders. Occasionally they invest the barroom to thaw themselves out in cold weather, and with a faint hope that someone will "set 'em up," but they seldom stay long, for they know they are not wanted by the proprietor, who hesitates not to make them aware of the fact, and the seeker after spiritual comfort, after taking a long last, lingering look at the array of bottles, secures his overcoat upon him with its solitary button, and goes forth again into the cheerless streets.

These unfortunates eke out a miserable existence in the winter time by transferring dark diamonds from the carts to the household coal bins, shoveling snow and doing odd jobs of all sorts, by which they manage to get hold of a quarter or so, and on receipt of the same betake themselves to a grog shop, taking care to choose one where a layout of pulpy and scoriac liver, yellow ochre-like mustard, and stale bread form the menu of the free lunch. How on earth they manage to exist at all during the long winter would be a deep and perplexing mystery, were it not from the knowledge of the fact that there is such a place as "Castle Green" on the banks of the Don, where a great many of them pass the happy hours away under sentences from "the colonel." In fact, too many of them. The jail is simply a harbor of refuge, to which they, by getting drunk or disorderly, can easily find their way, for notwithstanding the fact that these poor wretches have little comfort or enjoyment to look forward to in their hard journey of life, they prefer the cell and jail corridor, "skilly" and bread and water, and loss of liberty as well, to being half starved and in danger of freezing to death to the dignity of a few citizen.

Summer is the most propitious season for the bummer. When spring comes in earnest and navigation commences he changes venue from the inhospitable market square and its surroundings, and seeks the busy Esplanade with its outlying wharves where he, although not belonging to any organized stevedores gang, picks up a good many jobs in helping to load and unload vessels of all kinds, when he may be said to revel in comparative wealth, though his outward man is, as to dress, unchanged, for he, like many other philosophers, treats with scorn the vanity of dress.

CHAPTER XVII.
A VAG BY CHOICE.

A good many of these unappointed attaches of the stevedores have once been sailors and still have a hankering for the water side. A few days ago I met a good specimen of this class, who, although dressed in a dilapidated suit of "hodden gray," had the unmistakeable look of the sailor about him which needed not the "foul anchor" tattooed on the back of his right hand, nor the mermaid and other devices on his arms to confirm. I managed after a time to get into conversation with him, but the man seemed reticent, not to say surly. When I asked him if he had ever been to sea he replied, "Go to blazes and find out." I then told him that I meant no impertinence or harm by the question. I told him that I had a son now at sea, and consequently I took an interest in everything in the maritime line. To keep up the unities I took a plug of tobacco with which I had supplied myself with a view to just such an emergency, and offered the ancient mariner a chew, which he accepted and began to look a little more pleasant, and showed some signs of loquacity. I then proposed that we should go and have a glass of grog, a proposition which appeared to strike him as being correct. So we went to a water-side tavern sitting room where we each took what seamen call a throat season. I then suggested that we should have a smoke, to which the ex-mariner agreed, and another "throat season," which proposal also met his views. By this time my quondam friend began to wax merry, and went so far as to volunteer to sing a favorite song of his entitled "The Cumberland's Crew," a lyric based on the sinking of the United States war ship Cumberland by the improvised Confederate ironclad Merrimac at Hampton Roads during the Yankee "rebellion." I told him that, glad as I would be to listen to the heroic verse, yet it being rather early in the day to burst into song, I would much prefer to hear him tell me some of his doubtless many adventures that he had met with at sea. My ancient mariner at this stage of the seance began to get lachrymose, even unto the verge of tears.

"I don't like to speak or think of my past life," said he, "but if I tell you anything I may as well tell you all."

"Do so," said I. "I know it will be interesting," so I ordered some more grog and sat down again comfortably to listen to the story of the sailor tramp.

My partner drank his grog, laid down his pipe, took a huge chew of tobacco, and commenced his yarn. "I am neither a sailor or a sojer now. I am

NOTHING BUT A TRAMP,

although, by rights, I ought to be a gentleman. You needn't smile. I only said I ought to be one, but I am not. Yes, my father was a clergyman in the west of England. I won't exactly say where. However, he was rector of the parish, and I was his eldest son, and consequently the hope of his house. I had a younger brother who, I suppose, is at home doing well, at least he was when I last heard from him, but that's a good many years ago. Well, I may safely say that in all the west, east, north, or south of England, or, for the matter of that, any other country, there never grew up a more mischievous or incorrigible boy than I was. From the time I was first put in trousers until I got the bounce for good from my reverend father, I did nothing that I could help but rob birds' nests, upset bee-hives, and abet poachers and other bad characters in the neighborhood. I ran away and stayed with a gang of gipsies for six months, and the vagabond proclivities of my nature were remarkably well developed, as you can readily understand, in their company. A slight flirtation with a young woman, the particulars of which I need not mention, occasioned my hasty departure from the tribe, and I returned home a prodigal son indeed. I was then sent to Eton, where I attained a smattering of classics and mathematics, but as I unfortunately took the liberty of putting a quantity of cobbler's wax in one of the tutor's boots, and was convicted of divers other peccadilloes of like nature, I got my conge from my alma mater, and returned home again. My father, good man, got out of all patience with me, for my language was occasionally of the vilest, and I swore like our army in Flanders at the servants on all possible occasions. I was given a £50 note with a request that I would go forth and seek my fortune, which I did in London, but didn't find it. I spent all my money, and as a last resource shipped as boy on a drogher bound to Newcastle for coals. I was just turned sixteen then, and bitterly did I curse the day I tried the sea for a living. I was ropes ended by the skipper, thrashed by the mate, and kicked and cuffed by all the crew. This didn't suit me at all, so I stole the boat one night when I was on anchor watch, and sculled myself ashore, letting the boat go adrift when I landed, and tramped my way to Liverpool. I shipped as boy again on a Packet ship for New York, and on the passage I got it lively from all hands, they leading me the life of a dog. Well, we were all discharged in New York, and I shipped again, this time for Marseilles as ordinary seaman.

THE CAPTAIN WAS A TYRANT,

and the mates were even worse. All hands were pelted with belaying pins, and besides we were half starved. There happened to be a "tender" for a British man-of-war drumming up recruits for the English navy in the harbor, so I and two others put our shirts in the fire rigging (a sign that the officers of the tender well knew.) They sent an armed boat aboard, and I, together with about a dozen others, said we were British seamen, and volunteered to fight for the "widow," as the sailors call the Queen. We left in the tender for Malta, and were enrolled among the crew of the line-of-battle ship Brunswick, where we were put through our facings I can tell you. We commenced by giving cheek, but they soon took the nonsense out of us with the cat-o'-nine-tails. Well, to make a long story as short as possible. I was drafted into a corvette going home to Liverpool. I deserted on the first opportunity, and shipped again for New York. This was during the rebellion. I then joined the Yankee navy and arose to the high position of captain of the foretop on the United States frigate Essex. At Baton Rouge I was struck by a piece of shell in the leg, and sent to hospital, where I remained until the war was over, when I was mustered out of the service. I had a right to a grant of land from the government, but I sold it to a broker and spent the money for whisky. Since that time I've been knocking around through the States on the tramp. I can't ship before the mast, for my leg is so stiff that I am unable to go aloft. The only comfortable time I have is when I can manage to get into some hospital, where I get plenty of nourishment and a good bed to sleep in. However, here I am now, but where I'll be to-morrow the Lord only knows."

"Do you ever think of going home?" asked the scribe.

"Home! Well, I should think not. They, of course, think me dead long ago, and I don't want to disgrace them, anyway. My old father used to say, 'As ye make your bed, so shall ye lie,' or something like that. I've found it so, and must take the consequence." "Oh, I tell you," added the jolly tar, "there are thousands like me knocking around at sea."

"Take another bowl?" asked I.

"Don't care if I do," said the sailor. "There's no use being poor when a half a pint of

WHISKY MAKES YOU RICH."

"Well, see here, old fellow," said I, "I don't wish to be impertinent, but don't you think grog has been at the bottom of all your troubles?"

"No I don't," was his reply. "I never was much of a swizzer until lately. It's my own inherent vagabond nature that has made me the tramp I am. Whisky has been the ruin of many a good man, but I don't blame it in my case."

"Well, good-bye old fellow," said I; "I hope you'll strike luck some of these days."

"Good-bye," said the ancient mariner, and as I departed I heard him order another glass of the ardent to be drank au solitaire.

Here is one tramp, I mused, who appears candid enough, in all conscience, and who, strange to say, does not charge his decline and fall to the demon, drink. I could not help feeling a pity for this unfortunate, who, born in comfort and luxury, brought up at home and given every chance to get on in the world and lead a respectable life, had thrown himself away and become a miserable waif and wanderer. Mais chacun à son goût—Everybody to his taste. Some people have honors thrust upon them, but here is a fellow who deliberately heaps dishonor on his own unfortunate head. How many young men in the city of Toronto are, after a fashion, like this poor sailor? I know not their number, but I see samples of them every day.

Thus musing I strayed along the Esplanade,

While I chewed the end of a sweet and bitter fancy,

Until brought up all standing by the voice loud and commanding

Of a drunken seamen in a woolen "gansy."

I was about to tackle the seamen in the guernsey, or "gansy," as he would call it, with a view of learning something of his history, but as he, in answer to my polite enquiry as to the state of his health, told me to go to Halifax—or somewhere—and not liking his hostile looks, I concluded that I had enough of "Sailor town" for that day, and took a lateral traverse in the direction of the St. Lawrence market.

CHAPTER XVIII.
THE SLUM-DWELLER.

It cannot be said of Toronto, as it can be of some other cities, that whole districts are in such a condition as to be aptly designated slums. Portions of streets are inhabited by people whose manner of living is so degraded, and whose homes are so comfortless and filthy, as to merit such a term, but this cannot be said of any one whole district or street. Even Lombard street, which has rather an unenviable notoriety, has homes in it where the peace and satisfaction which crown industry and sobriety are to be found. St. John's ward, which is often alluded to slightingly, contains within its borders some of the handsomest streets in the city. Our merchant princes dwell there. Hundreds of mechanics make their happy homes in the Noble Ward. The slum portion is very small compared with the acres and acres where the domestic virtues go hand in hand with industry and plenty. Our city is of such a composite character that next door neighbors are often as far apart in their manner of living as is the east from the west. Strangers who read about the doings of the denizens of York street two years ago were surprised to find on visiting the city that there were many bright, busy stores, two fine hotels and plenty of respectable houses on the street. Any remarks in the following interviews regarding localities will therefore be understood to mean only certain portions of those localities.

INTERVIEWS WITH CLERGYMEN.

For the purpose of getting the views of a class of gentlemen whose profession brings them frequently in contact with the vicious classes of our city, NEWS reporters waited on several clergymen. Those selected were men who were known not to be shirkers from this unpleasant portion of a pastor's duties. The result will be found below.

A CITY MISSIONARY'S EXPERIENCES.

An evangelist and city missionary of some years experience in Toronto was interviewed. "You cannot," he said "tell what the Toronto slums are like, seeing them by day light. You enter a tenement house on Duchess or Lombard streets in the forenoon or at noon. All looks quiet enough. The women, generally of middle age, are standing at the door exchanging gossip with their neighbors. Some appearance of household work has been going on, and as noon approaches there is an odor of onion stew or fried pork. We enter. You are always safe in these regions when accompanied by a policeman or a reporter or a city missionary, but your visit would be much more favorably received if your escort be of either of the two latter classes. The furniture of the living room is of the cheapest and simplest description of second-hand ware, the tables are battered and sodden with the smear of innumerable drinking bouts. The chairs are evidently more often used as missiles propelled through the air by hostile hands than for the peaceful purpose of resting the human body. The crazy old windows are grimy with dirt; grimy are the floors, the ceilings, the ricketty stairways leading to unknown dens above. Almost all of these tenement houses are a perfect baby-burrow of children, untaught, unwashed, unkempt, enfants perdus of the gutter, the protoplasm out of which the great Sin and the yet greater Misery of our city is certain to shape itself in the future! Presently, three or four able-bodied young men come in from what they call work. A sinister-looking young woman in frowsy dress, the cut across her whisky-sodden face telling its tale of last night's revel, joins the group. The eldest child is sent with a cracked jug for beer to the corner saloon. As a rule, these people fare considerably better than the poorer ones among the respectable sober working people; they live from hand to mouth; the only text in the gospel which they obey implicitly being "Let the morrow take thought for itself." When they are not starving they are generally well supplied with bread, meat, tea and vegetables; nor are such luxuries as pies and cake unknown to them, to say nothing of malt or spirituous liquor, though, as a rule, the drinking sets in most heavily at night. At about 10 p.m. on Saturday or Sunday to see one of these establishments at full blast! Then

DRINK REIGNS UNCONTROLLED.

Of other immorality there is comparatively little; the scorching breath of the rum king will tolerate no rival! Money has been procured, if in no other way by pawning dress or tools to the people of the house, for every one of these tenement dens is, as a rule, an unlicensed groggery and pawnbroker's shop! The debauch which ensues nearly always ends in a free fight, in which the most furious combatants are often the women."

"Have you ever recognized in the night life of the city slums any man or woman you have known in better circumstances in this city?"

"Yes unquestionably, and in more cases than people would think who do not look below the surface for the three sorriest sins that enter hell, drunkenness, laziness and dishonesty, have the same effect on the educated and the uneducated. Take a recent case. Early last month I was called on to visit, not for the first time, a young married woman whom I had known in days when she had every right to the title of lady. I found her occupying a room on the rear ground floor of a house on Teraulay street. Her only baby, fortunately for herself and for it, lay dead. The father had more than once thrown it at the mother in a fit of drunken passion. I gave her money enough to provide decently for the funeral and promised to return two days afterwards, in order to conduct some simple sort of funeral ceremony.

"When I first knew this woman, then a girl years ago, her father was still living a prosperous hotel-keeper on Yonge street, a prominent church member, and an affectionate father who spared no pains on his daughter's education. Aggie grew up to be a bright engaging girl, with a charming figure, expressive hazel eyes, and long curling dark brown hair that reached to her waist. She was especially clever at ciphering, and acted for some time as book-keeper for a well known Toronto firm. She became an accomplished pianist, and sang for some years in one of our best church choirs. Her next misfortune after her birth in this evil world eighteen years before was her father's death. Her mother was left in fairly good circumstances, and the owner of a respectable house on George street. She was a good-natured but weak minded woman, the instincts of hotel-life were strong upon her, and as a matter of course, she took to keeping boarders. She kept a good house, and good table, for little Aggie was smart and looked after all that, and there were gay times when

AGGIE WOULD SING

and play for the young gentlemen in the evenings! But one set after another of young men came and went, and Aggie was unmarried at twenty-six, for bless you Sir, you know boarding-house flirts, as a rule, don't marry. Meanwhile drinking habits had grown on the mother, an inferior class of boarders came to the house. In an evil hour for herself Aggie became engaged to marry a handsome well-bred and well educated cadet of a rich Lancashire family, cotton manufacturers, whose trade brand is known through the world. Horace B— had been at Oxford for a few terms. A subaltern in a militia regiment which he had to leave, a clerk in the Civil Service, finally he was shipped off to Canada. He married Aggie and was a shiftless, reckless, drunken husband! Through him Aggie became addicted to drink, and her mother lost house and home. After many migrations they sought refuge in the Teraulay street tenement, where I found the dead baby. Two days later I renewed my visit. All trace of Aggie and her husband was lost, on a pine table the sole article of furniture in the room, lay the dead baby, purple with decomposition partly covered by a scanty rag! I learned from the people of the next house that a drinking debauch had taken place, the participants in which after hurling the furniture at each others' heads, threw the baby out of the rear window into the yard! I at once procured decent christian sepulture for this child of sin and misery.

IDLENESS AND DRINK.

The Rev. William H. Laird, pastor of Elm street Methodist church, stated that but a small part of his congregation, so small as to be inappreciable, came from the poorest part of St. John's ward, on whose northern verge this church is situated. Still he had visited among this very class a good deal, being led to do so by having particular cases brought under his notice by a young people's association in connection with his church, who had undertaken this duty. He was very frequently appealed to for monetary aid and to visit the sick and distressed. When asked if he had seen many cases in which reform had been effected through the influence of religious agencies, Mr. Laird said: "Yes, but only in isolated cases." He considered that the two great causes of pauperism were shiftless idleness and drink. The cases in which pauperism was the result of inevitable misfortune were, in his opinion, very few. The tramp, the beggar, the slum-dweller, owed his unhappy condition to one, generally to both, of the above causes.

RELEASED CONVICTS.

Among other clergyman of this city the writer was able to obtain the opinion of one who had been for some time acting chaplain of the Provincial penitentiary at Kingston. In reply to my question, "Have you seen anything of the Toronto ex-members of your convict congregation since your residence in Toronto?" this gentleman made the following statement: "I am glad to tell you that to my certain knowledge there are now living in Toronto no small number of reformed criminals whom I have known in the Provincial penitentiary during my term of office as chaplain. One of them is a tradesman in a small way living in St. John's ward. He has married happily, and is the father of several children. He is a most steady, sober, industrious man. I think great influence for good was exerted over this man by the introduction of church music into the penitentiary chapel, which, previously to my term of office, was not permitted by the authorities. The man referred to had a good voice, and was much interested in our singing classes, and since his release he has been a steady attendant at a Toronto church, of whose choir he is a valued member. Another one is that of a Scotch young lady, who had been decoyed to Canada by a faithless lover, and, as too often happens to girls not naturally vicious, had found her only refuge in a "fast house," having quarreled with the mistress of which, she was accused of larceny and sent for a short term to Kingston. Since her release benevolent ladies in Toronto received her and provided for her return home. She is the daughter of a missionary on the west coast of Africa, I also knew of several young men in quite respectable positions who have accomplished the difficult task of retrieving character and habits, even after touching the lowest depths of a convict prison. Certain forms of crime seem to me to be acute, like the most dangerous fevers which may kill, but recovered from do not recur. It is the smaller chronic types of crime, lying, thieving, drinking, which once contracted, hardly ever are eradicated.

"Do you ever recognize members of your former convict congregation who have not reformed?"

"But too frequently. Under the glare of Toronto lamps I see but too many faces once familiar to me in that unhappy flock of black sheep. I have recognized them among the loafers at the street corners, among

THE INCORRIGIBLES

half-thief and wholly drunkard, whom I have met when summoned to visit some case of illness or destitution in the city slums, I have seen the faces of women far more imbruted than when I had known them as convicts, and these not amongst the ranks of fallen women, strange to say, but chiefly as wives or housekeepers in rooms or tenement dwellings, in Duchess street or St. John's ward.

Once, shortly after I had ceased to act as chaplain at Kingston, I had left behind me still a convict, but under a promise of release for her good conduct, a Toronto girl named Annie —. Annie had been for some years a nurse in the prison hospital. She was singularly neat, good-humored, and devoted to her duties, and I was glad to hear she had been released. One evening in the July of that year, returning home with my wife to our house on G— avenue, what was my astonishment to see what appeared to be a bundle of rags huddled together on the porch by the door. With the dress of a scarecrow, with every appearance of exposure to wind and weather, with unkempt hair and all the appearance of a human wild beast, was the once comely and gentle Annie. We gave her a trifle to get a bed, and told her to come again next morning for breakfast and help, but she wandered away in the night and we saw her no more. There are many such women and men in this city who are never so happy as when in prison; the prison is to such a monastery, with its three-fold rule of poverty, obedience and temperance.

Of the criminal class in Toronto there are two grades; the first of these consists of those who commit the great crimes, such as murder, forgery and the like; such crimes result in many cases from motives which may occur but once in a lifetime; such cases of reform as I have seen have come mainly from these classes. But the crimes which depend on lying, dishonest, laziness, and unchastity are ineradicable, humanly speaking. The intenser forms of crime are like the deadliest diseases which attack but once in a lifetime; the other class of crime clings to the character like itch or leprosy.

Among the more famous Toronto criminals under my care was the famous

GRACE MARKS, THE GIRL MURDERESS.

She was a singularly beautiful girl, fourteen, with dark eyes, graceful figure, and a transparent olive complexion, when she and her paramour committed the crime, for which he was hanged. Grace had pleasing manners and though considerably past forty when under my care, still retained the remains of her girlish beauty. She told me that for many years she never slept without seeing the face of the murdered man in her dreams. She has been for some years a free woman, and is now a respectably settled married woman in an American city. There is one class of women who trade in human life, who are but too seldom brought within the grasp of the law, and when the guilt of murder is most clearly proven, are too often allowed to escape with comparative impunity. Perhaps the worst case of this class known in Toronto was that of the wife of an American quack doctor, to whom, and to her husband, was clearly brought home the death, by malpractice in their den, of a young girl, daughter of a minister of the gospel. I saw this woman-fiend in the workroom at penitentiary, pert, cheerful, and confident of the speedy relief she afterwards obtained.

FROM THE EAST END.

The Rev. Mr. Taylor, rector of St. Bartholemew's church, at the east end of Wilton avenue gave much interesting information with regard to the condition of the poorer classes at the east end of the city. "With us," he said, "there is more poverty than pauperism. What pauperism there is, unlike that screened from public view by the alleys of St. John's ward, can be seen from the public thoroughfares. The lowest district, Regent street, can be seen from Wilton avenue. It is wide and well-drained, but the humble hovels which line its sides make a hideous comment on its ambitious title. Little better than this is St. David's street, which crosses Regent street, east and west. Sumach street was poverty-stricken a few years ago, but is now improving, but Sackville, Sydenham, Parliament, and all the streets in this region are to a great degree peopled by the poorer classes of our citizens." As far as many years intimate acquaintance with the poor of this district has entitled him to form an opinion, there is little or no public immorality among those people, who thus form an entirely different class from the inhabitants of the St. John's ward slums. The great evil is a certain shiftlessness, a tendency to hope for support anywhere or from any one rather than to their own exertions. This I have noticed especially among immigrants from London and other parts of England. Mr. A. called on me several years ago with an introduction from one of the best known and most hardworking clergymen in a well-known London parish. He was respectably dressed, and though he lived in one of the poorest shanties in a lane off Sackville street, the place when I called there was clean, even neat, and decorated with a few good engravings and other survivals of his former English home. He had a wife, a neat, well-dressed person, three fine girls, and two as nice boys as I have ever seen. The girls had already found employment as dressmakers, a business to which they had been apprenticed at Camberwell, London. The father sought a genteel situation, something in the line of a clerk, bookkeeper or secretary; he could write a good hand, and was a competent arithmetician. But as you know, our city is already overstocked with applicants for such positions. I soon found that Mr. A. looked to the church for some slight monetary assistance, which, as our poor fund, small enough for legitimate uses, was already over-drained, I was obliged to withhold. The result was that Mr. A.

KEPT AWAY FROM CHURCH

for about a year. But the evil righted itself, as the boys grew up and found employment. They and their sisters supported the family by their earnings, an act of self-denial which, I have no doubt, was of the greatest possible moral benefit to themselves. After a time Mr. A. found occupation not wholly incompatible with his dignity, as caretaker in a furniture factory, became a most regular attendant at church and a communicant. This is the history of many of these English arrivals in Toronto, more especially of those who come from London. They are generally fairly well-educated, are respectably connected, and in most cases, I believe, are "assisted" to this country by relations anxious to shift from their shoulders the burdens of directing or aiding their course. The parents are people trained to earn money, if at all, in a single groove, seldom in one available in Canada. They cannot, like our people, turn their hand to anything that presents itself. But for all that they form a valuable element in our city population, for their children soon get Canadianized, imbibe the Canadian idea of being self-dependent and form the best possible addition to our vastly increasing numbers. One of the greatest evils I have to contend against in dealing with this class is an absurd and bastard pride and love of keeping up appearances. A woman living in a rented room on Sackville street lost a child by death. I provided her out of the poor fund with a plain black coffin as the means of conveyance to the place of interment. Soon afterwards another woman lodging in the same house lost a child. I offered to do the same for her that I had done in the former case. The woman indignantly refused, but begged me to give her money to get a more expensive coffin. Now, I had in my pocket a small sum of money from the poor fund, which I had intended to give her, but which I felt compelled to withhold when I found it would but be spent superfluously on "the trappings and the suits of woe." Still I felt sorry for the poor mother, in her desire to give a handsome funeral to her dead darling, though I could not conscientiously gratify her at the expense of those of my poor who needed food, not sentimental gratification. But when I came to officiate at the funeral I found she had provided a rosewood casket with white metal plate, a hearse and a carriage. Among my saddest experiences here are my visits to

THE NUMEROUS BABY FARMS,

which drive a more or less thriving trade in this part of the city. Some of them are situate on St. David street, several of them in a healthier position north of the General hospital. I have frequently visited these places; each dwelling will accommodate from three or four to as many as eight or ten infants, who are in almost all cases the children of shame, for whom their mothers, often persons in respectable positions, pay a small sum monthly. I do not think that they are neglected by the women who undertake the charge of them; in fact it is, of course, their interest that the babies should thrive, as on their living depends the monthly pay; but the circumstances of the birth and rearing of these poor infants, and, above all, the deprivation of the mother's milk, the often sour milk in the feeding-bottle, and the unavoidable crowding together, make these places nothing less than nurseries of death—the babies all die!"

CHAPTER XIX.
IN THE WARD.

My next interview was with the rector of a church west of Yonge street, the congregation of which, although attended by many of the elite in Toronto uppertendom, mainly consists of the lower middle class, and of the respectable inhabitants of the St. John's ward streets. In this church, as in a few others in the city, it may be said in the words of the oldest poetry, "The rich and the poor meet together, for the Lord is the maker of them all."

This clergyman does not wish his name published, but states his readiness to do so in a letter to THE NEWS should any doubt be expressed as to the accuracy of the facts reported.

The portion of Toronto from whence his congregation is drawn covers the poorest and least reputable part of St. John's ward—Teraulay, Elizabeth, and University streets, with the stretch of lanes and alleys between them, east and west; but north and south from these lanes extend smaller lanes, or rather rearages between the houses in the front streets, and occupying the place of the closets and woodsheds. In this network of slums comes and goes a fluctuating population of pauperism, the enfants perdus of the city, all those broken down by vice or poverty or misfortune.

One morning at the early hour of three this clergyman was awakened by a hard knock at his door. He put his head out of the first window and asked what was the matter. A man on the door-step said that his wife was dying, would Mr. — visit her? The clergyman hurriedly dressed, and accompanied his guide, who was far-gone in liquor, to a yard in the rear of one of the bye lanes alluded to above. As they entered the yard a number of small curs about the various premises began to bark, on which Mr. — beheld to his astonishment, several old wooden boxes gradually raised up, from each of which, like the head of a turtle from its shell, protruded the head of a boy who had chosen this strange sleeping-place, the bare ground for his mattress,

AN OLD BOX FOR HIS BED-CLOTHES!

Satisfied that no danger was to be feared, the unkempt little heads were withdrawn under their boxes.

They entered a room, full of men and women, on a table in which, covered with a scanty rag, was laid the corpse of the woman, who, the clergyman soon ascertained, had been dead for three hours. The husband, he shrewdly suspected, had asked for this visit in order to obtain drink-money, under pretence of assistance towards funeral expenses. The occupants of the room, male and female, were, most of them, more or less drunk; they belonged to the lowest type of Irish hoodlum; in the center of the room near the table on which lay the corpse, sat up a skinny old hag, repulsive and horrible in her mirth. Mr. A— was soon pressed for a small immediate sum of money, "jist to make things dacent." But my friend Mr. — is possessed, not only of great shrewdness and resolution, but has also the physical strength so necessary in visiting such dens. He refused their request for money, but said he would come next day and help. This kind announcement was by no means received with enthusiasm. The old crone in the bed exclaimed "musha, lave the gintleman alone; sure to-morrow we'll sind to the ladies at the convint, and it's they will do the dacent thing for us!" This appeal to the odium theologicum was judged to be ill-timed by the others, one of whom gave the old lady a dig in the ribs which sent her flying from the bed to the floor.

Next day he purchased a plain but neatly got up coffin at a cost of six dollars, with a shroud to match, and sent it to the house of mourning. But when this warm-hearted clergyman later in the day met the bereaved husband the latter broke out with "Arrah, tare 'an ages! did yer riverence think me woife'ud be buried in a thing like that, and she a rale lady born? Sure it 'ud disgrace the honor of the family!" On being thus rebuffed, Mr. — told the man

TO RETURN THE COFFIN

and its accompaniments to the undertaker. He learned that same morning that the widower's plea of poverty was, as it often proved to be with the occupants of those slum-tenements, a mere pretence. The bereaved descendant of Irish royalty had $12 due on that week's work, besides $39 in a savings bank. The man returned the coffin, etc., that morning to the undertaker, telling him that his reverence Mr. — thought it not good enough for the lady, and that a twenty-dollar coffin should be sent, along with a hearse and two carriages. For payment Mr. — would be accountable; the widower had agreed to repay him by weekly instalments. The ingenious ruse did not succeed, for the undertaker went straight to Mr. —. Whereon the disappointed and bereaved husband went on a week's hard drink. The body would have been left unburied, had not Mr. — ordered back the original cheap coffin and seen to the interment. This is the most typical case of one type of pauperism peculiar, I believe, to the lowest type of Irish and English paupers. It is not the opinion of this clergyman that such abject forms of mean and servile ingratitude are found among the most degraded class of our native Canadian tramps. It results from social conditions which exist in the old country but not here.

Another instance related by Mr. — illustrates what has been said already about drunkenness being at once the source and the solace of so many of the slum miseries; it is the atmosphere of their life, the pabulum on which they feed, the destroyer for whom they sacrifice wife, child, and finally life. The slum drunkenness is not that of the graceful orgies of an opera scene—it is terribly realistic, it is the sullen sodden ivresse of our Canadian rendering of L'Assomoir?

I proceed to tell Mr. —'s terrible but true tale of women drunk on the floor at a funeral. Mr. — was asked to undertake to read prayers at a house in a lane out of one of the streets in St. John's ward. On reaching the house he found every preparation duly made, a hearse at the door, a plain black-painted shell, with the body duly laid out within it on a table. The people in the room were

A ROUGH-LOOKING CROWD

of both sexes, some of them younger and apparently less hardened than the rest; all had been drinking heavily, but they received the clergyman with high good humor, which they carried so far as to interrupt Mr. — when he began the funeral service with groans, sighs, and remarks which were judged appropriate. Thus the versicle, "Man that is born of a woman is full of trouble." Mr. — was interrupted by remarks such as, "Thrue for yer riverence, and its meself knows it!" "His riverence is right, and may the hivens be his bed." All went tolerably well till Mr. — proposed to offer a prayer, and requested all present to kneel. Now all the assistants at this strange funeral were sufficiently sober to keep their feet, and had the Presbyterian ritual been observed, all would have gone well. The men managed to kneel—but the women, once they tried to kneel, lost the center of gravity and toppled over on the floor, whereon when Mr. — left the place, they were sprawling in the vain effort to rise!

The clergyman whose opinions I am now quoting was convinced that in slum-life there are many cases of guiltless, undeserved poverty, not due to drink nor to vice, but to other causes. As an instance of this, he told me that he had been informed that a poor, hardworking widow and her three little girls, living in a room in a tenement house on — street, were in a state of destitution. He proceeded thither at once. In a bare, unfurnished room, without a spark of fire, though it was February of a severe winter, were three little girls, each covered by a single ragged cotton garment. Their father was in a drunkard's grave; their mother, a frail, weak woman, was out of work. She could not earn enough to pay her weekly rent for that poor place and provide a loaf of bread daily for her children. It lay on the table ready for them to help themselves, but the poor little things had but little appetite. The youngest was five years old, the eldest seven. They lay in bed all day under the shelter of a single coverlet, for they had

NO CLOTHES, NO SHOES, THAT WINTER DAY.

The kind-hearted clergyman at once gave good food and fuel. Grateful warmth and nourishment followed in his wake, the little girls revived, and in the words of the Book, whose lessons his life is devoted to carry out, "The widow's heart was made to sing for joy."

A CHARLTON BILL CASE.

One of the saddest cases that had come under his experience this clergyman related to me as follows: It will be remembered that his parish includes that street stretching from Yonge street to College avenue, which may well be termed the vicus sceleratus, the Wicked Street, of Toronto. Several years ago a young lady visited him at his vestry, who was evidently in great distress. She had the manners and appearance of one who had been carefully and respectably brought up. Her story was soon told. Her parents held a good position in the town of —, Ontario. She was engaged to be married to a young gentleman of good professional prospects. Within a week of their appointed marriage, when the wedding trousseau had been provided, he forced the unsuspecting girl to yield to his wishes, then made an excuse for postponing the wedding day. After several months of this deception her condition necessitated flight. He took her to Toronto and placed her as a boarder in one of those nefarious "high-toned" fast houses where the Mother of Infamy entertains the daughters of death. When the girl found out the character of the place in which she had been left by her lover, who had now wholly abandoned her, she at once ran away, and obtained work as servant at a hotel. A day or so afterwards she was followed by the woman (the word seems misapplied) who kept the "high-toned" den from which she had fled. This wretch informed the poor, trembling girl that she knew her entire history, and would expose her if she did not return. Most unhappily the girl had not the presence of mind either to appeal to police protection, or to throw herself, surely not in vain, on the womanly goodness of the hotelkeeper's wife. She yielded, and became once more the slave of the procuress. She now appealed to the Rev. Mr. — for aid to escape

A LIFE WHICH SHE ABHORRED.

He gave her money to go at once to London and a letter to a kind-hearted Church of England clergyman in that city, promising to send further help on receiving news of her arrival. He heard from her several times. Two years afterwards he saw her again in Toronto, driving in a cab with two other girls. She turned her face away. Once more he was summoned to visit her. She was ill in a poor cottage on Elm street. For the last time he visited her, when on her deathbed in a wretched tenement on Teraulay street. She was dying, not from any disease, but simply from exhaustion, worn out with sorrow and despair. A name that is not her own is inscribed on the humble tombstone above her grave. Her parents, who are respectable people in good circumstances, have never known what has become of their lost daughter. "And the man whose selfish lust has brought about this ruin," said the Rev. Mr. —, as he concluded the above sad and over true story, "still walks the streets of Toronto prosperous and respected; still has the entree of the best Toronto society. I am a clergyman but there are times when I feel like taking a horse-whip and teaching that fellow a lesson which in this country can only be taught by lynch law. The Charlton Bill for making seduction a criminal offence, is necessary if private vengeance is not to be practically legalized. It is all nonsense to talk about the danger of black-mailing; a jury can always judge of facts and discriminate between cases of real moral turpitude and those which may be got up for the sake of money or intimidation."

A BABY FARM.

A Methodist minister of much experience among the Toronto poor corroborated to a great extent the views of his brethren. Among his more novel experiences the following was communicated in reply to questions about baby farming:

"Some of my most painful experiences have been in visiting 'baby-farms,' poor and generally narrow premises, for the most part situated in one or other of the slums. I think the popular idea about these places is erroneous—they are not intentionally shambles for infant lives, and poor as their accommodation for the little waifs and strays may be, are the only refuge of a vicious or unfortunate mother—a degree, at least, above desertion or infanticide! I was sent for last March to visit a sick child at one of these places, a cottage on St. David street, in the eastern part of the city. The cottage was a small frame building of but three rooms, in the largest of which, the 'living room,' were stowed seven infants, three playing about the floor, the rest in bed. Most of the children were pale and unhealthy-looking; they seemed to have none of the exuberant vitality of healthy childhood; even in their play they were languid. The little one I was called to visit was a child of six, whose pecky, shrunken face, large dark eyes, and unnatural development of forehead betokened the form of cerebral disease peculiar to childhood, 'water on the brain.' She was a gentle and intelligent little girl, and joined in the simple prayer I offered with a winning, gentle and tired, but earnest voice. It was her greatest wish to pass away from the world which had been to her one busy scene of suffering, unrelieved by any home or love beyond the casual kindness of strangers. A few days after my visit she sank quietly into sleep—her last. She was the illegitimate child of a young person in respectable position in society in a town of Ontario. Her mother paid regularly for her keep, but never visited her. Poor little Nellie! had her cradle known a mother's knee, the first symptoms of her sickness been met by a mother's care, she might have grown into a bright girl; affectionate and true I feel sure she would have proved. But perhaps it is best so, and the heathen saying, 'Those whom the gods love die young,' might be adopted as a motto by most baby farms."

CHAPTER XX.
A PEST HOUSE WIPED OUT.

It is the custom for people to say that evil has existed from the beginning, and will continue till the end of all things. And as far as anybody knows this is entirely true, but the application which a great many put on it is entirely wrong. They make the truism an excuse for ceasing all efforts for lessening evil and confining it to as few of our fellow-creatures as possible. When, some 18 months ago or more, a few gentlemen in the city got up a movement for the suppression of one of the forms of vice which, of all others, is the most degrading, destructive, and terrible in its results, they were met in the outset with the old saw, "This evil has always existed and will continue to exist." They did not propose to be put down by such an aphorism, and they pressed their ideas on the police authorities, the commissioners, and the magistrates until steps were taken to scorch at least, if not altogether kill, the viper. No one can deny one result which followed. Our principal streets, which were formerly thronged with wantons attired in purple and fine linen, became freed of them to such an extent that the presence of an occasional one caused remark. In the auditoriums of our places of amusement, where they were wont, like the Scribes and Pharisees, to occupy the prominent places,

THEIR PAINTED FACES

and flashing jewelry were missing. This was undoubtedly the result of a couple of months' work. It is well known that they left the city in droves. The heavy hand of repression has since then been removed, and once more the soiled doves flutter their plumes on all the public promenades. Two years ago York street was one of the worst streets on the American Continent. It would be impossible to conceive of lower dens or more desperate denizens than those who haunted the darksome cellars and holes on that street. There were dozens of keepers of these places, but a man named McQuarry occupied a bad pre-eminence above them all. McQuarry was an addition to our population which was contributed from rural parts. He had sold a farm and in some way or other lost the money in the city and started a store on York street. This store rapidly became a mere illicit drinking place and very soon was the resort of bad characters of both sexes. The state that the street had drifted into began to attract the notice of the newspapers, and the police also paid some attention to the phenomena connected therewith. The result was that raids were made on the places and severe encounters took place between the roughs and the officers. In one case an officer was dangerously stabbed, and the knife-user had his head battered pretty badly with the officer's club. Then the man with the phrase we have quoted above began to be heard from. You couldn't cure these things by drastic remedies. Evil always did exist, etc. A judge on the bench at one of the trials spoke in severe terms of the conduct of the officers. The prisoner, however, received a pretty severe sentence. The police kept up the war unremittingly, and the result was that at last York street was cleansed from end to end. A few of the old habitues still prowl about, and one or two dives have ventured to blossom forth again into existence.

In McQuarry's den it was the custom to hold a dance weekly, and these were perhaps

THE MOST DREADFUL FEATURES

of these wicked holes. A small fee was charged, but the proprietor depended more on the sale of bad liquor for his profits than on this admission. Many of the revelers had other business speculations in their eye, and woe be to the man wearing anything of value who did not keep all his senses about him, and even then he was not safe.

"Having paid my ten cents to a young man at the foot of the stairs," says an eye-witness of one of these orgies, "I descended into a cellar whose rough stone walls had once been whitewashed, but which were now discolored with the slimy moisture which oozed therefrom. The place was not large, and the 12 or 15 couple who were on the floor did not have much room in which to turn. Two colored lads supplied the music, one playing a very wheezy concertina, and the other tooting a fife. The company was largely composed of bad women and thieves. Here and there, however, could be seen a man who ought to be respectable, and who usually was accounted among his fellow-men as such. They were on the spree, and one of them, a master plasterer, I was told had been around the place for a week. He was sitting on a stone which had been pulled out of the wall, with a loathsome-looking creature seated on his knee. Among the

SCORE OF WOMEN

in the place there is not one who has one redeeming look of womanhood left. They have not that one trait which leaves a woman last—the desire to look well. Their faces are swollen with the fiery liquids they have been pouring into themselves all night. The men for the most part are not nearly so repulsive. The few "suckers" who are in the room, are doing all the treating, and as they produce their money furtive glances are exchanged, and that man's "roll" is spotted.

The company gets more riotous as the night proceeds and as the liquor begins to take hold. A fight starts in one corner of the room and all hands seem to join in. Pandemonium has broke loose.

"At once there rose so loud a yell

Within that dark and narrow dell,

As if the fiends from heaven that fell

Had pealed the battle-cry of hell."

Women and all join in the melee, and the cursing is terrible for its impiety and ferocity. At last the main combatants are parted, and one of them is carried upstairs almost insensible, with blood streaming from his chin, where his antagonist had rended a piece of flesh half off with his teeth. The victor swaggers about with the air of a conqueror, and his blood-covered fangs make even the boldest rough of them all tremble.

A girl entered after this, who took up a position near where I had squeezed myself into a corner to be out of the way of fists and boots, which were being thrown around loose a few minutes before. A glance sufficed to show that if she was vicious vice had not yet had time to mark her as it had the other creatures in the room. She looked a little frightened.

"They are having a good time," I remarked.

"Yes," she said somewhat doubtfully, "but I wish they weren't so rough."

I found out that she was a servant girl who had been out with her "fellow," and was unable to gain admission to her house. The knave or the fool had then taken her here. I ventured to suggest to her that this was no place for a respectable woman, and offered to go with her in search of a hotel, but as I found that she suspected my motives, I gave the matter up.

I found that a new piece of fun was being promoted by the humorous gentlemen of the house. They were carrying stories back and forth between two of the women, so as to

PROVOKE THEM INTO A FIGHT.

In this they were successful, and the two poor misguided wretches were soon screaming and clawing like cats on the floor. The men and women, howling and jibbering, formed a ring about this couple of unsexed beings. When the men were fighting the desire of every man in the room was to assist in parting them, but when two members of that sex, who are supposed to arouse in man all that is self-sacrificing and gallant, came to disgrace their claim to womanhood, these wolves not only stood by, but cheered them on to worse and worse shame.

"Come, my men," said a spectator, thinking to appeal to the better nature of some of the beings present, "stop this disgraceful scene."

But he was taken hold of and hurled against the wall with oaths. Bound not to witness what he could not remedy he made his way outside with a lower opinion of humanity than ever he had in his life before.

“I tell you,” said a friend the other day after the conclusion of the six days walk, “a man has more endurance than any animal.”

“Yes,” said the spectator of the McQuarry dance, “and he can be more brutal and more ferocious.”

CHAPTER XXI.
DOWN AT THE UNION STATION.

I never could understand what attracts people to the railway station. Go there when you will, morning, noon, or night, there are the same or similar lollers on the waiting-room benches, the careworn women, the crying children, the same sleepy-looking men, not forgetting the half-devoured buns, the rinds of oranges, and the peanut shells which litter the floor. Buns, oranges and peanuts, seem to have many admirers among those who go away in trains. Motion is the law of life, and nowhere does this universal decree of nature find a more striking exposition than at the railway station. I have seen many partings there, many warm handshakes, many tears, as I have seen many joyous meetings. I have seen men depart, with as much baggage as would fill an express wagon, depart amid the cheers of their friends, and I have seen the same men return poor in health and pocket, without a hand to welcome them or a cheery word to make them glad. I have seen men sneak up to the ticket-seller, purchase second-class tickets,

HIDE THEMSELVES

away in second-class cars, and go away unobserved. And I have seen the same men come back in a parlor car, rich in raiment and with many smiling, cringing friends to meet them. The railway station is the place to study people, from the tramp who rides in astride of the draw-heads of a freight, to the gentleman who occupies a section in the rearmost Pullman; from that bride over there surrounded by gushing, kissing, hugging friends, to that other party following long black box as it is wheeled away along the platform. The other night when I was there I saw a great, rough, but still kind-faced man sitting by the radiator, holding a sleeping child in his arms. She was wrapped in a red cloak, the close-fitting hood of which could not confine two tiny straggling curls. It was little Red Riding Hood taken from the picture, and in the grasp of a shaggy bear. With her head nestled upon the broad breast of the man and supported by a large, powerful-looking hairy hand, she looked out of place. Oh, where did such a man get such a child? He

COULD NOT BE HER FATHER,

for he was rough and powerful, while she was a dainty little thing whose appearance spoke of different surroundings from that of the man. He looked into the fair face with solicitude, and the unoccupied paw, heavy as it was, adjusted her cloak and fondled her as softly as a woman's. Then she opened her eyes, and out of the folds of her red covering crept a delicate little hand, upon which glittered a diminutive gold ring. It stole up to his hairy face and patted him on the cheek. Then the great big beard and the ferocious-looking mustache swooped down upon her and there was the sound of a kiss, and a childish ripple of laughter. I got into conversation with the man, when he asked for information in regard to the movements of the trains. He was going to Michigan, he said. Had a mill there, and was a lumberman. I remarked that the beauty of his child spoke well for Michigan. Not his child, bless her, his sister's child. Her father and her mother had died in a far eastern village in Canada, his native place, and he had come from his pineries to take charge of her. He was a bachelor, but, bless you, that would not prevent his taking care of his little charge. Oh, no, Dolly (so he called her) would never want for anything, and would be brought up a lady. I would have preferred that he had said he would make a woman of her instead of a lady, seeing that we have so many ladies and so few women, but I couldn't venture that freedom with him. For, whenever I hear of a girl being brought up a lady I picture to myself

A DAMSEL WHO PLAYS ON THE PIANO

a little, can dance a little, speaks French a little and English indifferently, and to whom the rest of the family and outsiders generally are expected to look up. As we were talking, a woman of the street came in and crouched on the seat near the steam-heater, for it was cold outside and frost had followed the sunshine. Little Red Ridinghood noticed her poor bedraggled look, and sidled up close to her.

"Are you a poor woman?" she asked in a feeling way.

"Yes, a very poor woman, God help me," I heard the forlorn creature reply.

"Would you take some money from me?" and Red Ridinghood fumbled for her little pocket, and having found it dropped a piece of money in the woman's hand.

"Won't you shake hands with me?" she asked as the little one was moving away.

"Oh, yes, if you are a good woman," said Red Ridinghood, loud enough for all to hear.

The hand-shaking did not take place, for just then a train rushed into the station, and Dolly's uncle, learning that it was the train he awaited, called her, and lifting her in his arms, he nodded to me and hastened towards the platform. Just before he went out the little red hood popped over his shoulder, and a childish voice cried out:

"Good-bye, poor woman."

I looked at the "poor woman" to mark the effect of the farewell. She was leaning towards the heater, with her chin resting on her hands. There was a bitter expression on her face. I thought I saw a tear glistening on her cheek, but before I could satisfy myself as to this good sign she rose abruptly and left. I saw her slink through the crowd, the scoff of men and the scorn of women, away along the platform, through the archway, out into the dark streets, amongst the lost whence she came.

CHAPTER XXII.
MORE ABOUT THE UNION STATION.

The vast, smoky building facing the Esplanade between York and Simcoe streets is a great theater in which are enacted some of the strangest scenes in life in this city. Through it day and night a tide of human life with all its joy and misery, with all its wealth and poverty, flows continually. East, west and north, day and night, trains go thundering on their way, infusing fresh blood and vigor throughout all the land. The station and its surroundings are like some mighty fort stocked with inexhaustible supplies, sending out hourly sorties against the unlocked resources of a great country, and coming back triumphantly, laden with spoil for the enriching of the nations. At almost any hour of the day or night the scene at the Union station is an interesting one, especially to the student of human nature. Here are to be seen people of all nationalities, Canadians and Americans predominant of course, but in the busy throng can often be seen Swedes, Norwegians, Italians, Greeks, Hungarians, Danes, Germans, Spaniards, Frenchmen, Gipsies and Jews, mingling strangely under the great roof. The most interesting scenes are those witnessed on the arrival and departure of the great express trains for the east and west. Early in the morning the big express for Montreal and all points east leaves the station. For an hour beforehand the yard men begin to "make up" the train and the people arrive. Sitting patiently on their dunnage bags and rough boxes in a corner are a group of

FRENCH CANADIAN LUMBERMEN

on their way home to Quebec from the Michigan pineries. Their faces are all bright with the expectation of being so soon back with the old folks at home, all bright, expectant and happy, save one, who sits with his chin in his hands and a look of sadness on his swarthy face. And why? Because Baptiste, his young, his only brother, who had accompanied him to the woods full of strong life and hope had been struck dead by a falling tree not a month ago, and lay in a nameless grave beneath the dark shadows of the Michigan woods. And this has taken all the joy and light from the homecoming of Louis, who is wondering how he will face the old mother at home and tell her for the first time of the tragedy which has robbed her of her best-loved child. The crowd begins to thicken along the platform. As I walk down through them I notice a party of prominent politicians in a group, and on enquiry I learn that they are a deputation to Ottawa for the purpose of interviewing the government, which will doubtless take their suggestions into its most serious consideration. Here is a portly merchant on his way to Montreal to look after large consignments of goods, and to the last moment is closely attended by his clerk, to whom he continually pours forth instructions. The nobby gentleman, nonchalantly smoking his cigar as he coolly paces up and down, is a

COMMERCIAL TRAVELER

about to launch himself on the unsuspecting country merchant. He has just seen that his cases of samples have been put on board, he travels according to the commercial tariff, the little leather bag contains luxuries for the trip, and he feels perfectly confident and at home. He chats with the conductor, nods to the brakesman, and offers a cigar to the porter of the Pullman. As he stops to adjust his glasses, he rolls his cigar in his mouth and looks up at the murky ceiling with the air of a man who is ready for anything or anybody. These young fellows you see there are students on their way home. By their looks they have spent their last night in Toronto in great shape, and even now they appear somewhat enthusiastic as they pace to and fro arm in arm. Here is a lady bound for the distant burgh of Oshawa. She is loaded down with flower-pots and parcels. She is red in the face, and her nose is sharp. She is industriously trotting up and down after an official. The official is industriously scurrying here and there to keep out of her way. Finally, by a skilful flank movement, she captures him, and with an air of triumph, enquires:

"What time does the 7.45 train go out, sir?"

"At 7.45, ma'am."

"Will it go out on time?"

"Sharp on time."

"D'ye think I would have time to go up to Smither's store before it starts?"

"Depends how far it is," and the official dashes off on an imaginary errand to escape further questioning, while the lady mentally makes up her mind that she will write to the papers about the discourtesy of these officials. Soon all is bustle and ferment. The old lady is hustled here and there in a sad way. The elbow of a porter knocks a twig from one of her plants, and she immediately sets up an outcry, which is successfully drowned by the rumbling of

THE BIG BAGGAGE-CART,

filled with luggage, which comes lumbering along the platform, making a lane through the throng. People out of breath come dashing into the station, and make a bee-line for the ticket office regardless of all obstacles. The gong sounds. Its discordant notes start the throng into livelier motion. More people arrive out of breath and somewhat excited. A married couple plunge along dragging a train of children after them, who are continually getting between people's legs. The conductor walks up and down beside the train, answering questions pleasantly, and nodding and chatting to acquaintances. More people arrive. The last of the baggage has been passed into its especial car. The mails are on board. Most of the passengers are in their seats, and, bare-headed, are leaning out of the windows viewing the scene without. The gong sounds again, and then a tall, red-whiskered man, with a voice like a fog-horn, calls "A-a-all-l-l, aboard for Belleville-lle, Kingston, Montreal-l-l, and a-a-all-l points east." The rest of the intending passengers make a rush for their seats, there is hand-shaking through the windows, a pretty girl standing well back kisses her hand at a certain window, the conductor sings cheerily, "All aboard!" the locomotive goes "Toot, toot! fizz-whizz, fizz-whizz!" the great wheels revolve, and the morning train for the east is gone.

CHAPTER XXIII.
THE NIGHT EXPRESS.

The lights are burning dimly in the Union station—they never burn brightly in a station, somehow—and it is an hour before the night express starts on its noisy triumphant journey west. Down the vista of the long platform a couple of noisy young women are sauntering. Their peals of laughterless laughter—if I may coin an expression—ring through the resonant place. The baggageman, who knows me, beckons me to a seat beside him on a big iron-bound truck, and remarks that the girls are here again.

"Do they often come here?"

"Almost every night, and others, too. They are respectable girls for all I know, but the Union station has a fascination for them somehow. They flirt with the brakemen and the Pullman car conductors, and sometimes make a mash on a young swell from the country as he comes off the train. They are mighty sharp and shrewd, I tell you."

"Hullo," said I, looking behind me, "is that a coffin?"

"Yes," said the baggageman carelessly,

"THAT'S A COFFIN

with a stiff in it. Come down from Winnipeg this afternoon and no one has come around to claim it yet. There's lots of 'em nowadays. They're coming an' going all the time. We shipped one chap to San Francisco last night. They are a horrible bother. Wonder what they want to do it for. This stiff is bound for Milwaukee. If they had buried him here he would have heard Gabriel blow his trumpet as plain in Toronto as he would in the Western States. They're a most mighty bother."

"I should say so," said a train hand standing near. "I'll never forget the experience I had with one."

Seeing the look of interest on my face, he blew the ashes off his cigar and continued:

"I was runnin' on No. 4, from Hamilton through to Detroit and one dark night they put a stiff aboard at Harrisburg. That was all right, but when they put another aboard at Paris I felt they were givin' it to me too much. I was alone in the car, and tho' I ain't scared of ghosts and that, yet I didn't feel just to home. There's no fun in ridin' along in the dark with a couple of stiffs, now I tell you. There I sot, and for the life of me I couldn't keep my eyes off them coffins. There lay two dead men with their wooden overcoats on, and there I sot smokin' my pipe and feelin' ornery. Something got loose under the car, and the knockin' underneath sounded to me as if one of them had come to life and was tappin' on the lid of his coffin fur me to let him out. You needn't laugh, it was no joke. It was a ride I'm not going to forgit in a hurry, either. Well, I pulled through all right, an' run into Detroit in the mornin'. A hearse was drawed up, but when we got the coffins out we found that the label cards had been knocked off, and we didn't know which was which. We couldn't ask the stiffs themselves, you know. One old man came up, and with tears in his eyes said he wouldn't like to plant anybody in his lot but his own blood relations. Well, we opened the coffin, and I hope I may die if it wasn't plugged plum full of smuggled silks and laces."

"No stiff in it at all?"

"Stiff! naw; but the other stiff was the genuine article, and the old man driv off after it in great shape, as happy as a clam, yes, sir."

"Did they ever find out who smuggled the goods?"

"No; but they never tried that trick on again, that I know of."

Here I noticed a detective sauntering up and down the platform.

"Well, John," said I, "what's on to-night, anything up?"

"Just wait a while and you'll see," with that wise and knowing air which only a detective can assume. At that moment the headlight of the locomotive drawing the train from Hamilton appeared at the west end of the station, and the detective suddenly became very alert. He stood midway on the platform, and as the train came to a standstill and the passengers came pouring out he scanned the features of every one who stepped upon the platform. Suddenly he made a swift little movement, dived through the crowd, dodged round a kissing and hand-shaking group and

LAID HIS HAND ON THE SHOULDER

of a middle-aged man, accompanied by a young woman. I was quite close by, and couldn't hear what was whispered in his ear, but the change that came over that man's face was something terrible to see. He turned white, then red, and finally a greenish yellow shade settled on his wild and drawn face. Like a boy caught stealing apples he whined, "let me go, let me go; oh, for God's sake let me go." He shook like a man with ague, and he would have fallen only the detective's firm hand sustained him. The girl by his side was, as far as outward appearance was concerned the most self-possessed of the two, but her startled eyes and pale face told that she, too, was suffering. A curious crowd had gathered round, from which the detective skilfully extricated them, and then the trio made their way to the Central station. They were searched, and a large quantity of money found on both of them, but the girl was allowed to go to an hotel, while the man, weeping like a baby, was taken down into the cells. He went down like a drunken man, stunned, helpless, miserable. The story may be interesting. He was a country storekeeper, influential, respected, trusted. He was a Sunday school teacher, he led at prayer-meeting, he was a delegate to conference, he was grand patriarch of a temperance lodge, he conducted family prayer in his house morning and evening, in fact he was looked up to as a model man. He had a wife and six children. The former was sickly. He engaged a girl young and inexperienced in the world to assist his wife in household work. She attended his bible class and looked up to him as

A SUPERIOR BEING.

He wasn't a bad man as the world goes, but he was not a strong man morally. He and the girl made a mistake, he, because he was morally weak—she because she believed that he could do nothing wrong. From that hour he began his downward career. He borrowed, embezzled and even stole money, and one afternoon by a preconcerted plan the pair took the train for Toronto. Deluded wretch, swift as went the train bearing him away, he thought forever, from the scene of his misdeeds, a tiny wire string along the track bore a message swift as thought past him. So swift indeed, that a detective had time to go home, eat a quiet supper, and walk leisurely down to the Union station and smoke a good cigar on the platform while waiting for the victims that were sure to come. And all this time the pair were sitting in the railway carriage planning schemes for the future, and never dreaming of what was before them. The man was sent back to his own county for trial, and the girl's father came down a few days afterwards and took her home.

The express going west had made up by this time, and the crowd on the platform was thickening. Cabs and omnibusses rattled down York and Simcoe streets and drew up on the Esplanade front. A large group of well dressed people, flowery with buttonhole and hand bouquets, smiles, and laughter came sweeping in. In the center of the group is a handsome girl, with flushed face and unnaturally bright eyes, whose every motion is nervous and constrained. She is neatly dressed in a brown traveling suit and holds a superb bouquet in her trembling hand. By her side, with a self-satisfied look of proprietorship and triumph, stands a gentleman who glances with no little impatience in his eyes, first at the train and then at the group around him. But with the first clang of the gong

THE PARTY GROWS QUIETER.

A constraint falls upon them. With the clang of the discordant note the bride turns pale, and a wild look comes into her startled eyes. She trembles visibly, for in this train her new-made husband is to bear her off to a strange land among strangers. All old associations are broken to-night, all her old loves and delights are cut from her, the faces and scenes so dear to her she may never see again, she will never be to those about her what she once was, and all to go with this man for better, for worse. They put their arms around her neck and kiss her till all at once she bursts into an uncontrollable fit of weeping. She clings to them desperately till, led into the car, she folds her arms about her husband, now her only hope and stay, her father, mother, brother, counsellor, companion and friend from this time onward and forever. A man with hat over his eyes darts into the station, buys his ticket, and has his foot on the steps when my friend John, the detective, taps him on the shoulder and smilingly says, "Not to-night, Dickey, my boy, you must come up to the station and explain some things first." Who is this leaning on that old man's arm. A young man

GOING HOME TO DIE.

His face is white as death and almost transparent, his eyes are fearfully bright, his fevered lips have shrunk from his dry, white teeth, his body is emaciated, and his step is feeble and slow. Going home to die! Not two years ago he came to the city, robust and strong, full of life and hope; to-night he is going home with his poor old father to die in the arms of his mother, who is waiting, waiting, waiting for him in the old farm-house far away.

"See that old chap there with the glum look?" whispers John, the detective.

"Yes."

"Well, go and interview him; he's been cleaned out by confidence men."

I went up to the old gentleman, and after some trouble got him to talk. He was spitting tobacco juice right and left in a vicious manner, and his lower jaw was chewing away as if it went by clock-work. His tuft of iron-grey beard fairly wagged with righteous indignation.

"I was a standin' on the platform here this aft'noon, a-waitin' fur the train to go home, when two right-smart young fellows kem up, an' sez they, 'Hillo! old John Hess, what on airth air you a-doin'?' Got the advantage uv me,' says I, 'don't know yah!' 'What,' sez they, 'don't know old man Turkman's nevies?' Sez I, 'Be you Levi Turkman's sister Maria's boys eh?' Says they, 'why of course,' an' we got a-talking about Toronto and politics, an' religion, an' the crops, when who shud come up to one of 'um but a man who wanted pay for freight, er somethin' er another. Well one uv these chaps pulls out a hundred-dollar bill, but the man sed he couldn't change it no how. They then asked me to lend them the money, $69.47, and I

COULD KEEP THE $100 BILL

till we went up town and changed it. I forks it out convenient like, and tuk the $100 bill, and the three of um went off to see about the freight, an' I haven't seen a sight on 'em since."

"And the $100 bill?"

"Ain't worth shucks! and they ain't old man Turkman's nevies no more nor you be. Ef I had the consarned cheats here now I cud lick a ten-acre field full on 'em. Bin a huntin' all over town fur 'em, but 'taint no use. Dang the town ennyway."

Here comes a lady with her dear little boy—one of those dear little boys who makes the ordinary traveler just ache to spank him.

"Maw!" he says, "where you goin' to?"

"I want to see the conductor, dear."

"Maw! wot's a conductor?"

"He has charge of the train, dear."

"Maw! wot does he do that for?"

"For a salary, dear."

"Maw! wot's a salary?"

"Oh, dear, don't bother me."

"Maw, w'y won't you let your little boy bother you?"

"Hush, I want to speak to the conductor."

"Maw, wot you goin' to speak to the conductor for?"

"I want to know if the train stops at Guelph."

"Maw, is that where my gran'paw lives?"

"No, he lives in Goderich."

"Maw, wot does he live there for?" and so on endlessly.

The crowd thickens, the gong strikes, the cheering "all-aboard" of the conductor is heard, and in a few minutes the night express is darting like a meteor through the darkened land.

CHAPTER XXIV.
THE EMIGRANT TRAIN.

It seems that when the rain is falling, when the air is chill, when the darkness is deepest and when the great station looks most gloomy and dreary, the emigrant train arrives. As the train draws in and slowly passes me to its allotted space the faces that I see through the dirty windows are tired and worn and the eyes are hollow and sad. I went through an emigrant train one night and I will never forget the experience. The emigrants were chiefly Irish, English and Swedes. Some of them stayed here in Toronto but the majority were bound for points farther west. As I opened the door of the first car a blast of hot, foul air smote me in the face and almost turned me sick, and yet the people whom I saw before me seemed to mind it but little. They were used to it and it was a great improvement on the poisonous atmosphere of the steerage. The car was closely packed, every seat had more than its quota. It was impossible to see to the far end of the car on account of a steam which fermented the place and made the faces of people in the middle of the car look obscure and distorted. The emigrants were in every attitude and conceivable posture; some were lying prone on the floor, others were huddled in the seats, while others, with arms entwined, were resting their heads on each others' shoulders. One whole family, man and wife and six children, were squeezed into two seats in the most amazing manner. The parents formed a sort of under strata on which the little children were piled promiscuously. They were all asleep,

THEIR ARMS ENTWINED,

their cheeks touching, and their spirits winging through dreamland back to the good land of Sweden far away. Utterly unconscious of their surroundings or of the great city into which they had entered, ignorant of the fact that they had halted at one of the chief stopping places on their journey, they slept on, and as I watched them and saw their lips move and the unintelligible words drop forth, I knew that they spoke of home. One poor man with bowed head was weeping quietly, and I asked him what ailed him.

"Oh, sir, she died in Monthrehal."

"Who died in Montreal?"

"Me wife, sor, the voyidge killed her sor; oh, wirra, wirra, why did I bring her away."

Three little children were clinging to his knees and looking up at me with wondering eyes. The man glanced up through his tears, which he struck from his eyes with his shut fists.

"Sure I'm better off than that poor crathur yonder—go an' shpake to her, sor."

The woman he pointed out was sitting alone in her seat. She was young and good looking, but her face was drawn and pinched with some sudden and bitter woe. Her baby was wrapped in a dark shawl, lying very still, and she rocked it gently in her arms, and talked to it in cooing voice.

"Is your baby sick?"

"No sir."

"It is sleeping then?"

"Yes sir, my baby is sleeping."

A little girl who was on her knees beside the woman lifted the shawl from the sleeper's face. The baby was dead! The mother looked up with

A QUICK SHUDDER OF FEAR,

and with a world of pity in her startled eyes.

"Oh, sir, don't tell them, they would take my baby away, and he would never see it."

"Who would never see it?"

"It's her husband she manes," said the sympathetic emigrant at my side. "He sint fur her from Michigan. The wee choild was born after he left, and she wants to bring him his baby dead or alive, poor craythur."

"When did it die?"

"This soide of Kingston, sor. Shure the railway min don't know it yit, and there she has been houldin' that dead baby in her arrums ever since."

"I want t' let him see it, sir; I want t' let Miles see his baby," and bending over the little dead body the hot tears fell on the somber shawl.

In a far corner with their arms about one another, and with her head lying on his breast, sat a young married couple who were going west to seek their fortune. What a strange bridal trip! She was in a troubled slumber, but he was painfully awake. Finally she awoke and looked about her with an expression of alarm on her tired face, but when her eyes met his a swift smile of gladness chased all fear away, and she nestled her face on his shoulder again, and clasped her arms about his neck.

"Jim," she said, softly, "I was dreaming of home—I thought I saw the old bridge, and the chapel on the hill where we were married, and I thought I saw mother comin' down past the boreen, and she was callin' to me, 'Katie, Katie, where are you, asthore?' and it wakened me."

The girl sat erect, looking straight in her husband's eyes. "Jimmy," she cried, "take me home again." A look of pain swept over his face. She saw it, and with a woman's swift repentance she flung herself upon his breast and was silent.

A look of utter weariness bordering on misery sat on one and all.

"Well, this is the divil's own counthry, to be sure," said a very surprised and somewhat frightened-looking immigrant to me.

"How's that?"

"Ye see that wee gurrul sittin' there?"

He pointed to a Swedish girl who looked as if she had been crying very recently.

"Well, be me sowl, it's no loi, but a mon kem aboard awhile ago, and while the craythur was asleep he stole her beyootiful yellow hair wid a pair of shayers, be gob!"

"It seems to have frightened you?"

"Thrue for you. I saw a man on the platform above wid only wan leg, an' bedad it wouldn't surprise me if he tried to shtale one av moine."

I jumped off, laughing at the fellow's downright uneasiness, and in a few moments the train drew out from the sheds.

CHAPTER XXV.
THE WRECKING TRAIN.

In the morning, as I have watched the conductors, engineers, and trainmen trooping down to the Union station, and marked one of them, a fine, hearty, lusty, fellow, I have wondered if he would ever come back. A collision, a pitch-in, a broken rail, or a low bridge are possibilities always before them. I was in the Union station one afternoon when a wrecking train came in from the east, bringing the crew and portable parts of a train which had been wrecked by a pitch-in away down the line. Four of the train-hands, including the engineer, had been hurt, some of them seriously, and to see the fine young fellows, all broken and hurt, lifted out of the car to be sent to the hospital, was most sad. On the platform stood an old woman, who, on seeing her boy borne out, broke into bitter weeping.

"Oh, Johnny, Johnny, my boy, my boy! Didn't I always want you to keep away from them awful trains? Don't take my Johnny to the hospital. I'll nurse him—indeed, indeed, good gentlemen, I can nurse my Johnny better than anyone." Then the subtle woman rose up in her. "Is his face hurted? Will he be disfigured? No, thank God! Oh, but he was a pretty boy."

"How did it happen?" I enquired.

"Freight train ahead of us lost her grip on a grade. The brakes wouldn't hold and she broke away and run back and we pitched into her."

"I suppose your engineer stuck to his place?"

The train hand smiled a superior smile.

"You bet he did; catch Bill leaving his post while there is any show to do anything."

One man had his leg broken, another had his breast crushed, the engineer had sustained fatal internal injuries, and Johnny had his shoulder crushed. These things don't bother railway men much. In a few months after all hands, with the exception of the engineer, were back at their work again as devoid of fear and careless of consequences as ever.

CONDUCTORS' EXPERIENCES.

"There is a sameness about our lives which makes it monotonous," said Conductor B—as he lit a cigar and reflectively tossed the match into the gutter.

"Yes, but you have a variety, surely."

"Yes, but this variety becomes the regular thing, and I tell you it gets monotonous; still what we see may perhaps be worth reproducing in print.

The latest thing that I remember as peculiar is this: I noticed a well-dressed, middle-aged lady on the train every day going to Toronto and coming back. She was as regular as clockwork, always wore the same highly respectable clothes, never had any baggage, always sat alone and never spoke to me. She made the trip with us every day for two weeks steady and I began to get interested in her. Just when I was getting thoroughly puzzled as to who she could possibly be, she disappeared."

"Well."

"Well, she was a mad woman, that's all. As crazy as a bedbug and this railroading was a mad fancy. She broke out bad at last and they had to put her in the asylum. It makes me cold to think of what she might have done had she broke out in the car."

"Have you thrown off any tramps?"

"Oh, that's an old story and we get used to it by degrees. I remember one thoroughbred, however, who was a dandy. I was running from Hamilton and I found out he had neither money nor ticket, so I put him off at Waterdown. I thought that settled him, but in going through the cars I found him on the rear platform, looking as comfortable as you please. I jilted him off at Bronte and told him that if he got on again I would paralyze him. When we reached Oakville the station-master told me that a man had ridden in on the cowcatcher. I went forward and caught my joker sitting on the pilot smoking a clay pipe.

I FIRED HIM OUT

of that, but when I was collecting tickets for Mimico I found him sound asleep in a cushioned chair in a first-class coach. I kicked him this time, but when we got to the Queen's wharf he jumped down from the top of one of the coaches and disappeared in the darkness. Oh, he was a thoroughbred, I tell you. When I was a freight conductor I used to have a lot of trouble with them. I soon was able to distinguish between the regular tramp and the poor fellow who was in a hole and trying to get home to his friends. That kind of a man I would give a lift to, but the others, you bet, I give them the grand bounce every time. I have caught them riding astride of the bumpers; I have caught them under the car swinging by the rods; I have caught them in the bonded cars, in the cattle cars, anywhere they could get, and always bounced them. They are a funny crowd."

"Have you much trouble with gamblers and crooks on the cars?"

"Not much now, but we used to, though. The line from Detroit east is still infested with them. They are confidence men and three-card monte players chiefly. You know what three-card monte is, and how it is worked, don't you? Well, one night a man rushed into the car where I was and told me he had been swindled at cards. I went out, and when I entered the coach where the deed had been done three men rose from their seats, darted to the other end of the train and jumped off. We were going at the rate of forty miles an hour through a rough country, and I was sure they would be killed, but I never heard of them after—they escaped by a miracle. On another division of the road, however, a gambler jumped off and paid the penalty of his crookedness by breaking his neck."

CHAPTER XXVI.
MILLIE'S FIVE CENT PIECE.

While looking over his exchanges the other day THE NEWS editor clipped from the Switchellville Recorder a two-column article with five headings, the first of which was "Kidnapped," in flaring letters. The article, dealing as it did with an erring woman, who had fled to the city, seemed to him to touch in some way or other the night side of city life, and in that connection interested him. It led off as follows: "Man is born to trouble as the sparks fly upward, but few are called upon to bear as much trouble as our wealthy but unfortunate fellow-townsman, Mr. Switchell. All will remember when he brought home to his handsome residence a beautiful wife. None will forget the advent of his little daughter. Everyone was sorry when he was prostrated with fever, and recovered only to find himself almost entirely deaf, or "very hard of hearing," as the phrase goes; but the climax of sympathy was reached two months ago, when his young wife, after eight years of married life, grew tired of her deaf husband and eloped with Dr. Clarke, a man who has only been known to the people of this village one year, but who in that time has contrived to swindle almost every one of them. But a still greater blow has fallen upon him. His little daughter Millie, who had all her mother's beauty combined with her father's integrity, and a certain sweetness of her own, has disappeared. The neighboring country has been diligently searched, without result, and the conclusion is inevitable that the child has been kidnapped by her

BEAUTIFUL, BUT ERRING MOTHER.

No one who knew Millie will wonder at it. The only wonder is how the mother could have lived so long without her; but the sympathy of all will be with the deserted husband and lonely father. Poor little Millie! The villain Clarke will soon desert her mother whom he has already debauched, and she will drift into a life of still deeper shame. Pure as Millie is, she cannot but suffer from contact with such associations. It is this thought that has almost driven her father crazy. Oh, if men and women, before yielding to evil impulses, would remember that the little children must suffer for it, what a different world this would be."

The article was continued to much the same effect through two columns. As the NEWS editor finished reading a letter bearing the Switchellville postmark was handed to him. It was from THE NEWS correspondent at that place, and read as follows:—"Read the Recorder for big sensation. Since the Recorder was printed a domestic in the employ of Mr. Switchell has confessed that she bought a ticket for Toronto at the request of the child, who was determined to go off in search of her mother." THE NEWS editor said to himself "If the wanderings of that child could be followed up they would make an interesting addition to the gaslight scenes."

"Whatcher cryin' about, little girl?" said a red-haired, freckled-face, ragged boy, with a bundle of papers under his arm as he looked sympathetically at a well-dressed little girl who was wiping away with her handkerchief

THE TEARS THAT HAD ESCAPED

from her eyes despite a brave effort to keep them where they belonged. "Whatcher cryin' about, is yer lost?" "No, I'm not, but my mamma is. A bad man lost her, and I'm trying to find her for my papa and me, 'cause we're homesick without her."

"Where do yer live?"

"Away, way off. I took my money from my little savings bank, and Mary bought a ticket to bring me to Toronto. She said everybody came here, and she guessed my mamma was here. I've just got five cents left."

"Bully," said the boy, "that's just enough. If you want anything you can get it by advertising in THE NEWS for five cents."

"Where's that?"

"You just go down that street there until you come to the winder where all the picters is, and that's THE NEWS."

"How many papers do you want, little girl?" said a clerk in the business office of THE NEWS, as he put his head through a wicket to take a five-cent piece which a child was holding up.

"I don't want any papers. I want my mamma," said the child.

"Your mamma isn't here, little girl. What is your name?"

"Millie Switchell, and I come to Toronto to find my mamma, but it's so big I'm almost lost myself."

"So you want to put an ad in THE NEWS, do you?"

"Will that find her?"

"Perhaps so."

The news editor had entered the room while this dialogue was going on and he

RECOGNIZED THE CHILD.

A dispatch was sent to her father, and before he arrived Millie was persuaded that the better way would be to allow some one well acquainted with the city to continue the search. The father on his arrival said: "It may be asking too much, but I wish you would suppress the names. If you must tell the story call me Switchell and the village Switchellville. The people in my neighborhood will understand the case just as well with those names, and very few of your other readers will know that the names are incorrect. I am sensitive enough myself, but would ask no favors were it not that the publication of names might have a bad effect on the child's future."

Sympathy got the better of journalistic instinct, and the real names do not appear.

CHAPTER XXVII.
THE JAIL.

The jail is a place towards which the night-hawk gravitates as naturally and as irresistibly as Newton's apple to the ground. They disappear for a season, and when they resume their operations in the haunts of men they will tell you that they have "just put in a month," or more, as the case may be. The corrective influences of jails is a much debated point, but there can be no doubt that men are admitted to the jails or other penal institutions who learn such a lesson thereby that they determine that their first taste of such a thing shall also be their last.

The writer remembers getting a very graphic account of his experiences from a gentleman who is still living in the city, and who dates his reformation from habits of insobriety from a police magistrate's commitment to prison. The gentleman will of course recognise whose pen traced these lines, but as his name will not appear in the course of the story, and as his fate may serve to "point a moral and adorn a tale," the liberty is taken of reproducing his confidences as nearly as possible in his own words.

"From my eighteenth to my twenty-third year I had been gradually piling up for myself a taste for "bumming." After business was done in the store I could not rest in the house at night, although I had as pleasant a home as ever a young man had. My sisters devised all sorts of schemes to interest me and keep me at home. At tea-table, without seeming to wish to inform me of the matter, they would be discussing among themselves

THE ACCOMPLISHMENTS AND BEAUTY

of some young lady friend of theirs whom they expected there that night. But it was all to no purpose. I had made the acquaintance of a gang of fellows and I can only describe myself as being infatuated with their society. If I had been compelled to stay away from them for one night I think I would have burst. I have often thought the matter over since and I have come to the conclusion that my liking for the society of these fellows lay in vanity. The most of our evenings were spent in saloons, where we drank and talked, and sometimes sang. I always did my best to amuse and please, and it was very flattering to my vanity to find that I was apparently successful in doing so. My companions laughed and applauded whenever I spoke. I will not say how much their smiles were inspired by the round of drinks which was sure to follow an unusual burst of laughter.

This way of spending my evenings soon began to tell its tale. I became a source of sorrow and anxiety to all my friends, and as I became more addicted to liquor I decidedly descended in the estimation of my employers.

Formerly all my drinking was done at nights; now it became necessary for me to take an "eye-opener" in the mornings, and finally I drank all day long, taking all sorts of excuses to slip out and have a nip. I tell you honestly, Jack, there is no sort of liquor sold over a bar whose taste I like. I know of no drug that is more distasteful to my sense of taste and smell than the strong liquors, whisky, brandy, gin, rum, and I can't say much better of beer. Yet I used to pour all these down my throat, concealing as much as possible the wry face I was inclined to make at them. I found myself at length out of a situation. I now

DRANK HARDER THAN EVER

to drown my chagrin. Even at this day, when I look back to that time, I experience a sense of humiliation and shame that makes me fear to look my fellow-man in the face. I never yet preached a temperance sermon to any man; perhaps because I feel I have no right to, but I say to you that I am firmly convinced that drink deadens everything that is best in man. Let a young man be distinguished for his domestic affections, for gratitude, for chivalry to woman, or any other noble quality, and then let him take to drink, and as sure as night succeeds day piece by piece these virtues will vanish from his character, and be succeeded by brutal indifference, selfishness, and weak wilfulness. During these years my family viewed my decadence with almost silent grief. My mother would sometimes gently remonstrate with me after I got very bad, but it appeared as if I could not stay myself. I frequently woke in the morning and found the clothing and boots, which I knew had been mud-bespattered almost beyond redemption in the debauch of the night before, brushed and tidied into respectability once more by my sisters' loving hands. This touched me so that I determined to do better, but the resolutions were mighty sickly ones, and seldom outlived the day. I was six months out of employment, and during that time did nothing but waste my days in taverns, sulking about like a criminal until I got enough liquor in me to make me feel bold. Oh, when I think of that six months my blood boils. Sometimes I was away from home for two or three days at a time.

ONE NIGHT I GOT "PULLED IN"

by a policeman, and woke up next morning a prisoner in the cells. But I did not know that fact when I woke up. I was lying on a hard floor, but that did not surprise me, as I had frequently had that as a waking experience. I looked about me for a few minutes, and found that I was not alone in the room. Several other men were lying on the floor. The stench in the place was sickening. "Where can I be?" I said, and I tried to recall the events of the night before. Just as I was trying to do so the chimes of St. James' cathedral rang out, and like the thrust of a cruel sword the thought darted through my head, "My God, I'm in the police cells."

I must have been still full of liquor, but that thought brought consciousness and soberness at once. I sat up against the wall, and oh, what bitter thoughts thronged through my brain! In spite of me, the great hot tears welled from my eyes. The hero in the Silver King, which I saw at the Grand, says, "O God, roll back Thy universe, and give me yesterday!" These were not the words I used, but that was the thought. Oh, if I could only have avoided this last dreadful crowning shame of all! But, sir, I thought things in that cell that have saved my life. It was a bitter experience, but it has proved salutary. I could tell you every thought I had from the time I woke in the morning until I was put in the prisoners' dock a few minutes before ten. One prayer was predominant in my mind, and that was that my people would never hear of my disgrace. I was assured by my fellow-prisoners that, it being my first offence, I would be discharged. Well, I was brought into the court and placed in the prisoner's dock. I had an idea that I presented an appearance of respectability in contradistinction to

THE FROUSY BESOTTED WRETCHES

who were my companions in misery. But nobody with whom I came into contact gave forth any sign that my appearance was not in consonance with my position. The policemen pulled me here and there with as great disrespect as if I were the veriest bummer. I at length recognized that I was not only a bummer but that I looked like one. When I was asked to stand up I did so, and while I was engaged in wondering what the great gaping crowd of loafers in the court thought about me, a man had testified that I had broken a window, and the magistrate imposed a fine of $1 and costs or twenty days' imprisonment. I could not quite understand this sentence. I knew I hadn't a cent in my pockets, but I could not believe that for lack of $4 I would suffer the indignity of imprisonment. Oh, it could not be. It was a wild, improbable dream. But the drama moved on with relentless step, and presently I and a lot of other miserable creatures were driven into the jail van like a lot of dumb brutes. There is no use in dwelling on my feelings. One hopeful feature of my case was that I did not blame anybody but myself. As I thought what and where I might be and what and where I was I kept repeating to myself, "Yes, I am insane." I said that a score of times, and thought I could offer good evidence in support of the assertion.

The van swept in at the jail gate and landed her vagrant load on the stone steps of the imposing institution. Our names, occupations, religious belief, etc., were entered in a book. Dinner was over before we got there and the new arrivals had to wait till supper-time for food. This was no deprivation to me, as I could not have eaten a Delmonico dinner, let alone the bill of fare prepared by a prison cook. We were searched and sent to our corridors. In the one to which I was assigned there were about a dozen fellows, mostly young, who treated me with more

CORDIALITY AND FAMILIARITY

than was agreeable to me. A turnkey came in, however, soon after and took them all out with the exception of myself and three or four others. I was then left to commune with my thoughts. I had not been in the prison half an hour before I was not only willing but anxious that my friends should know of my whereabouts. I shall go mad if I am left here over night, I thought. Then I reflected that someone who knew me would see my name in the papers and that I would soon be rescued from my horrible position. I felt that if I stayed there twenty-four hours I would lose my self-respect beyond recovery.

One by one the hours of the afternoon wore away. The suspense in which I was held during that time was unbearable. Every step on the stair made me hold my breath and almost stilled the beating of my heart. If any one looked in at the grated corridor door their features assumed the shape of some one of my friends. At length those who had been working outside came in and soon after we were marshalled out and proceeded in Indian file to supper. I fairly loathed the thought of food, and the chunk of bread and pannikin of pasty porridge which were the only articles of the menu, unless you include water and salt, were not calculated to tickle one's fancy. There were no tables, the benches on which we sat having to be utilized for both table and chair. Interpreting my look of disgust, my right and left hand companions shared between them my supper, much to the disgust of the fellow behind me, who said he had asked me first.

Immediately after supper we were locked up in our cells for the night. That was my night of nights. Up till midnight I did nothing but

LISTEN WITH STRAINING EAR

to every sound of the great building. Through the high dome, off which the corridors run, even a foot-fall echoes with funereal hollowness. In the early part of the night the door-bell rang very frequently, and at every peal my heart rose in my throat. "That must be them," I kept repeating, but as each time I was doomed to disappointment I began to give way to despair. About midnight I lapsed into a peculiar condition of mind. I was quite awake, but half of the time I thought there was someone in the cell who, although he said no word, yet I knew to be sneering at my mental promises of reform. I had not expressed to him any promise of reform, but I thought he could read what was in my mind, and he thought me a coward. My anger at this would occasionally rouse me out of this hallucination, but again and again I lapsed into it. How I hated this accusing, sneering being whom my distempered fancy had conjured up. Murder was in my heart towards him. I have thought over my experiences of that night until I can go through the whole series of my thoughts as readily as I could through the scenes of some familiar drama.

About an hour after daybreak a bell was rung, which was a signal for us to get up and dress and tidy up our cells. A procession of male chambermaids carrying slop-buckets was then started for the yard. This duty being done, we were marched in to breakfast. I was not hungry, but I was weak and trembling in every limb. I knew that this was the effect of want of food, and I determined to eat something whether I felt like it or not. When I found, however, that

A POUND OF DRY BREAD

and unlimited water and considerable salt was the bill of fare, my revolted appetite refused to be led into such pastures. As before, my rations were eagerly seized by my fellow-prisoners.

When Turnkey Allan came in for the working squad after breakfast, he chose me as a member of it. This frightened me almost to death. I had visions of men working on the roads in chains, and I said tremulously that I wasn't able to work. "Oh, you'll feel better outside. You won't have to work very hard." So out I went wheeling a barrow with a pick and shovel in it. The squad were engaged in taking clay out of a bank on the hill beside the jail, and were wheeling it down to the road. No one who has not undergone captivity, can understand the feelings of a prisoner. It was a lovely summer day this, and as I looked from the brow of the hill up and down the wide-reaching valley of the Don, I could not believe that I could not obey my own inclinations, but was bound to submit my goings and comings to the will of the two turnkeys who were in charge of the squad. I was very weak, and I thought my heart must break.

"Here, B—," said one of the turnkeys named Norris, "take hold of this wheelbarrow."

They were very considerate to me, giving me very small loads of clay, but nevertheless in half an hour my hands were so blistered that the handles of the infernal vehicle seemed as if they were red-hot. At length I fell on my knees from pure exhaustion—prostrated in mind and body.

"He's not able to work," said one of the other prisoners.

"Let him lie on the bank," said one of the turnkeys to the other. "He'll be better out here than inside."

And he was right. I lay in the warm sun, and presently began to experience a feeling of hunger. Just as I was experiencing this hopeful sensation I heard some one say on the bank below, "Where is that man B—?"

MY HEART GAVE A GREAT THROB,

the blood rushed into my head, and everything swam before me. I did not swoon, however. I was taken back to the jail by the turnkey, who had been sent for me. There I found my sister talking with the deputy-governor. I could not speak; I shook her hand. I was taken upstairs and had my own clothes restored to me, and in ten minutes was walking down the hill. The evulsion of feeling was so great that I had no sense of shame. I simply felt like a new man—and I was. That jail experience of mine was the turning point of my life. I determined to stay right in the city here and live down my disgrace. For six weeks I went out every morning and looked for work, but without success. I returned to my home every evening and stayed there. It was very discouraging, and required all the resolution I was capable of to keep myself from slipping back. One day I went to my present employer. I had heard that he wanted a junior bookkeeper. I told him my whole story. He engaged me. That was over five years ago, and I am there yet."

CHAPTER XXVIII.
THE STREET ARABS.

The night-hawks of a great city like Toronto are not confined to men and women. Boys and girls, and even children of more tender years, fill a place in the ranks. They are, therefore, deserving of some attention, which I intend they shall receive. The poor homeless, friendless little outcasts, who make the street their home because they haven't a better one to go to, are those of whom I wish particularly to speak. They are the sport of chance and the children of misfortune. They find themselves in the midst of the stern battle of life, fighting for an existence, years before the children of well-to-do parents have taken the first step toward preparing themselves for the fray. It is not a matter of astonishment that the majority of them grow up to become part of our criminal population. The wonder is that any attain to good citizenship, as not a few have done.

THE WAY THEY LIVE,

and the things they do, are matters which most people know but little about, and seem to care still less. Most of them start out as newsboys, bootblacks, or both combined. Those who don't turn out to be thieves and "toughs" learn trades, and sometimes develop into shrewd and successful business men. Let me tell you about the doings of some of the street arabs of Toronto that I have known. Their names I won't mention, though I have them all before me, because I hope to see some of them occupying a better position in life one of these days. In that case it wouldn't be agreeable to them, perhaps, to have somebody turn up the files of THE NEWS and remind them of the adventures of their boyhood.

First I will tell you about the good boys I have known, for as I have said, in spite of their poverty they are not all bad.

About fourteen years ago one of the best bookbinders in England emigrated to Canada with his wife and little boy. They settled in Toronto. Shortly afterwards the man commenced to drink. His wife soon followed his example. They both went down the hill rapidly. Finally they drifted into prison, and their little boy was left to shift for himself. He experienced hard lines for a long time. Like the sparrows, he got his food wherever he could find a crumb, and slept under a crossing, in an empty packing-box, or elsewhere as fortune might decide. When a reverend gentleman, who had known his parents under better circumstances, took an interest in the lad's welfare, and went in search of him, he found him

IN A MISERABLE HOVEL

in St. John's ward. His fellow-occupants were lying in the worst stages of scarlet fever, and had he been allowed to remain longer with them, he would probably soon have been beyond the need of his friend's assistance. The gentleman procured lodgings for him, and started him in business as a newsboy. He continued nearly two years in the business, and then obtained a situation which he still holds. His father died in Toronto jail and his mother in the General hospital.

A little fellow, whom I know very well, was thrown upon his own resources by reason of his parents quarreling, and afterwards separating and breaking up their home. He got a job in a well-known Toronto shoe factory at $2 per week. In the middle of summer business became dull, and all hands were given a month's holiday. Now there were things that Jimmy needed far more than a month's holiday, namely, shelter, food, and clothes. He saw that something must be done. He bought a stock of newspapers, and went to work to sell them. His bright face and industry brought him success. At the end of the month he had paid his way and saved $27. He sent a $5 bill to his mother, who was in the country, to come home. When she came back he gave her the balance of his money to furnish a couple of rooms. Soon after she was reconciled to her husband, the boy went back home to live, and ever since harmony has reigned in the household.

I am sorry that there are not more examples of this kind and less of those which follow.

TIM AND SAM.

"For ways that are dark and tricks that are vain,

The Toronto young vag is peculiar."

Wee Tim Mc— and his pal, Sam W—, are aptly described by the above couplet. They are the best known of any of the hundreds of young urchins who pick up a living on our streets. Though scarcely more than 10 years old, they have had a short residence in every charitable institution in the city. In every case their evil genius tempted them to say and do things which could not be tolerated by the managers, and they were dismissed. Now they would find it impossible to get admittance to any of the places mentioned, even if they so desired, which they don't. Time has hardened them. During the latter part of the winter just closed Little Tim was a frequent applicant for shelter at one or other of the police stations. One night, between 11 and 12 o'clock, a policeman's attention was attracted by a child's sobs. A search in the darkness revealed Little Tim lying under a street crossing, without coat or shoes, and shivering from the cold. His association with the officers of the law and the police cells has stripped them of their terrors. He no longer trembles with fear at the sight of them, and the power which once deterred him from wrong-doing has but little influence upon his conduct. He does not hesitate, when opportunity offers, to appropriate

WHAT DOES NOT BELONG TO HIM.

Several times he has had interviews with the Police Magistrate on account of such offences. In almost every instance, his tender years and pitiful face procured for him immunity from punishment, but it is doubtful if he will be able to evade justice much longer. Little Sam, his bosom friend, and the sharer of his adventures, has a home to go to, but he prefers to be a rover. His forte is begging, at which he is very successful. His method is to hang around the doors of the principal restaurants and coffee houses. When he sees someone approach that he thinks he can deceive, he instantly begins to sob as though his heart were breaking. The unsuspecting and kind-hearted stranger stops and enquires what his trouble is. He replies, as he vainly attempts to stifle his sobs, that he hasn't had any breakfast, doesn't know where he can get any, and is all broken up with hunger. A dime, or sometimes a quarter, rewards his stratagem, and he goes around the corner to laugh in his sleeve at the clever fraud he has perpetrated. Not long ago Sammy's career was near being closed up in a rather peculiar manner. He had stopped out late, and knew it was useless to go home, so he crawled into a half-filled ash barrel, and was soon sound asleep. Presently a couple of scavengers came along and dumped the barrel upside down into their wagon. Poor little

SAM WAS WELL NIGH SMOTHERED

before the scavengers became aware of his presence and extricated him from his uncomfortable position. It is said that since that little adventure he prefers a packing box or the shelter of a street crossing to anything in the shape of a barrel. Sammy's confidence in his pal seems to have weakened of late, judging from a remark which he made to the Police Magistrate the other day. He said: "When I've got money Tim sticks to me, but when I haven't he tells me to go to the d—l."

Last September eight boys belonging to the Newsboys' lodging became imbued with the ideas of Tom Sawyer. They pooled their spare cash, hired a sail-boat, and made the voyage to the island. While there a storm arose, and they were afraid to attempt the return trip, so they erected a temporary shelter, and camped out over night. The next day they reached home, half-frozen, their clothes soaked with the rain which had poured down upon them during the night. The ring-leaders were sharply reprimanded for their conduct. In consequence of this they left the institution, and prevailed upon about twenty of the other boys to follow their example. For a couple of months afterwards, the boys slept in the old bolt works building on the

Esplanade. The hardships and exposure which they underwent told heavily upon them. One returned to the lodging with a severe cold, which clung to him and

ENDED IN HIS DEATH

a few weeks ago. Another lies suffering in the hospital at the present time from the same cause. In spite of all this, many of these boys prefer to sleep on the street rather than be subjected to any restraint.

Some of them have a roving disposition, and take periodical excursions to other cities in Canada and the United States. I know some who have more than once visited Chicago. One boy's father told me that he came from England to Canada simply because in the Old Country he found it impossible to keep his thirteen-year-old son at home. The lad hadn't been long in Toronto before he ran away, got aboard the train, and stole away to Montreal, from there he went to Quebec, and thence to Chicago. His father is now living in the neighborhood of Lambton Mills. He doesn't know where his truant boy is, and has given up all hope of ever getting him back home again.

I could go on for an indefinite length of time, giving incidents in the lives of Toronto street arabs. The examples I have cited will be sufficient, however, to enlighten those who have never troubled themselves to inquire into the circumstances of these children of adversity to whom the lines have not fallen in pleasant places.

CHAPTER XXIX.
THE HOSPITAL.

That a good deal of the ailing and suffering endured by humanity is superinduced by vicious habits of one kind or another is a pretty well ascertained fact. The staff of the General hospital could inform you that many of the "cases" who pass through their hands owe their debilitated or broken frames to excess or neglect of one kind or another. The General hospital, therefore, is, as well as the jail, an institution which the battered and enfeebled sinner resorts to when he can no longer stand up against the world's buffets. You will find them there, the children of slothfulness and inebriety. Charity refuses to condemn them for faults which have their root in that weakness which is to a greater or lesser degree inherent in our common humanity. She has declared that their wounds must be healed, their quivering nerves steadied and their wasting vitality in general restored. This is done at the general hospital without money and without price. As many as are able to pay their way do so, but lack of this world's goods does not preclude ailing mortality from shelter, food, medicine and healing.

The fretfulness of people who are ailing is well known, and every once in a while one hears of

COMPLAINTS AGAINST THE MANAGEMENT

of the hospital, either privately poured into a friendly ear or more publicly expressed in the daily papers. All of our public institutions are subject from time to time to this sort of criticism, and perhaps it does no harm, although doubtless it is galling to those officials, many of whom labor hard and long to render their establishments as perfect as possible. But perfection eludes the sons of men, and an approximation to it is all that can be looked for, even in what is called a "model establishment." No doubt the medical superintendent at the hospital has many difficulties to contend against, and if he might speak out in meeting and let the people know what they are, more sympathy and credit would perhaps be awarded him.

At night the hospital looks like a building illuminated on a gala day. From each of its many scores of windows a beam of light cleaves the night shadows. If you cross the portal at this hour the first person you are likely to meet is a kindly-faced woman in a coquettish spotless muslin cap, plainly dressed, with that pure complexion which very generally distinguishes women who are much indoors and whose health is good. This is one of the night nurses. She might stand for a picture of the Goddess Hygeia—with modern trappings. One would half forgive fate for making him sick to be tended by such an embodiment of "sweetness and light." All must agree with the opinion that it is a great point to have the attendants on the sick, persons whom it is pleasant for the eye to rest upon.

This young woman whom I have been speaking of goes up stairs and noiselessly glides down a ward. She carries a lantern, whose soft light, however, does not wake even the lightest sleeper. She passes two or three of the little cots, and at length arrives at one where

AN OLD MAN LIES.

He has a white bandage about his chin. She scrutinizes his features, and then passes on. Her last instructions before going on was to keep a watchful eye on this old man. He is a farmer, and a few days ago he was admitted to the hospital suffering from cancer. A great bunch of the devouring ulcer was seated on his left jaw. After examination and consultation among themselves the doctors told him that if it was allowed to remain there he must die; if, on the other hand, an operation was performed, he might live. They asked him to choose. He chose the operation. His vitality was low, and the surgeons knew that the chances were greatly against their utmost skill. They do not like a case like this. The probability is so great that the operation will merely hasten death, that it is an unpleasant one. Medicine is of no avail in this case. He is fed entirely on a milk and spoon diet. The operation was performed yesterday afternoon. After the old man recovered from the ether he lay in a state of stupor, breathing hard. In the evening the doctor saw him and shook his head, and then gave the night nurse explicit instructions regarding him.

The gas in the ward is turned down to a blue spark. Everything is very still. Not even a snore is heard. Snoring is generally the result of gross and heavy feeding, and the jaded appetite of the sick helps them to avoid gormandizing. Every five or ten minutes the nurse leaves her chair in the corridor and passes down the ward with her little lantern. Sometimes she gently awakes a patient to apply a poultice or cooling lotion. She always looks at the old man. At length she makes a longer pause and seems

DISTURBED BY WHAT SHE SEES.

The old man is breathing stertorously. Half of the eye-balls are hidden under the upper eyelids—the whites are turned up, and make a ghastly continuation to the white bandage round the chin. The nurse moves hastily away and summons one of the assistant physicians. Everybody else in the great still room is asleep, and in its pale light no token is given of the presence of the angel of death, but before the physician's return the dread work is done, and the old man's troubled spirit has passed into the land of shadows. The calling of the date was merely a matter of form. Everything is done quietly. No one is wakened. A screen is put about the little cot. Two stout men are summoned from below. The corpse is pinned up and carried away through the silent ward.

CHAPTER XXX.
PIECES OF MEN.

The convalescent patients at the hospital are not only permitted, but encouraged, to take full advantage of the two greatest remedies in nature's pharmacœpea, fresh air and exercise. On the west side of the main building, a long, substantially built stairway leads from the various wards to the recreation grounds below. Here are planted trees, grass in abundance, and benches here and there for the double purpose of rest and shade. A little north of the center building and the fever hospital is the convalescent-room, a large, airy building, furnished inside with lounges, tables, chairs and the appurtenances for such simple games as draughts and dominoes. The upper story is devoted to the use of female patients. On fine days, however, the majority of the inmates prefer a pipe outside. Although many of them are destitute of funds, few appear to suffer from want of the magic weed. There is a sort of freemasonry among smokers, and the stingiest of men has scarcely the heart to refuse an occasional handful of tobacco to his more needy fellow-sufferer. And how some of the poor battered wrecks enjoy the luxury, even though the pipe be a short and rank dhudeen, and its contents the dryest and most bitter of five-cent plug!

That man in the blue coat, reaching nearly to his knees, is a notable example. He is

THIN AND HAGGARD,

and his ghost-like aspect is heightened by the sleeves pinned up at the shoulders of his dilapidated garment. If you ask him, he will tell you he has not six inches of arms to his whole body. He was knocked down by an engine some months ago while he was intoxicated. He fell length-wise, with an arm extended over each rail. To him the pleasure of an occasional pipe is perhaps enhanced by the difficulty which attends the obtaining of it. It is quite a little study to watch how the poor devil goes about the process. Some kindly patient, acceding to his request for a match, places one between his lips. The maimed man hops joyfully off to a second, whom he has noticed to be the possessor of a fine T. &. B. plug, almost intact. Somebody fishes the suppliant's pipe out of his pocket, fills it with the crumbled 'baccy, and, less fastidious than most readers would care to be, places the dirty stem in his own mouth, and with a few sturdy puffs, sets the contents glowing bravely. And now the armless man, his cutty fairly inserted in his lips, stalks off to an adjacent seat, secure of happiness for at least one sunny half-hour. Perhaps, mutilated as he is, and past sharing in what most men deem the active enjoyments of life, his mind is more at ease now than it has been for many a day. His eye has lost the old

FURTIVE LOOK OF THE TRAMP,

who never dared to strengthen his supplications by a straightforward gaze; he is no longer a wanderer and homeless vagrant on the face of an earth whose spring-time blossoms had no message for him or his kind. He has forgotten already the cold nights passed in the streets or in the parks; the questionable benefit of a troubled sleep in some frowsy ten-cent lodging-house; the pitiful struggle, reversed day after day, to obtain enough food to keep soul and body together. For the rest of his life he doubtless counts on being beyond the reach of actual want. He will be cared for by some of our benevolent societies and received into some charitable institution where the balance of his chequered life will be quietly spent, undisturbed by thoughts of a past which had nothing in it worthy of regret.

That man on the veranda is an old soldier. Like most of his class, he delights in nothing so much as to gather around him a little crowd of patient and interested listeners. He still cherishes a fine

CONTEMPT FOR CIVILIANS,

slightly modified by the present exigencies of his condition, which involves certain obligations to the despised class, in the way of tobacco and such like minor accommodations. He has been in India, Afghanistan, Abyssinia, Zululand, and last, but not least, the Curragh of Kildare. Curiously enough, it is of this last that his reminiscences are most lively, and its recollections are evidently cherished more lovingly than those of foreign lands. If he tells you anything about these last, you need not hope to hear much of unfamiliar customs, of strange sights, of hair-breadth 'scapes; your old soldier is seldom a great observer or a graphic reciter of stirring events. Barrack-room pranks, guard-room escapades, and long dialogues with officers, in which the narrator invariably comes out ahead, are the staple of his talk. His wooden leg does not seem to cause him a moment's trouble, and he tilts it up on an adjacent chair as jauntily as if it were a souvenir of Isandhula, instead of a legacy from a drunken brawl in front of a Lombard street shanty. It is to be feared that this ancient warrior is a bit of a fraud; but he is such a light-hearted, garrulous, transparently mendacious old party that one is not inclined to be too hard on his shortcomings.

This old man whom you saw move into a chair a minute ago is suffering from no specific disease. Behind the tightly drawn skin can be plainly discerned the lineaments of the fleshless skull. As he sits his eyes are the only features that save the face from being a perfect likeness of that of a corpse. When he moved to this seat his movements reminded you of a very jerky automaton, so stiff were his limbs and so wooden his body. I do not know one fact about the history of this old fellow in his shabby garments, but certain I am that if it were skilfully treated there would be from it than from any one of the numerous "lives" of great men which flood the book stores. "Failure" is written in every wrinkle of his clumsy clothing and in the sad lines of his face. It seems to me that the life history of such a failure would be as interesting as the details of a career of one whose whole life might be summed up in the word success. But the particulars of the existence of such men are buried with their bodies in the odd corner of a churchyard, and we can only guess at the foolishness, the blunders and the sins which have withered this man's life. As I said before, this specimen of hospital flotsam and jetsam is suffering from no particular or specific disease, and there are a dozen around these grounds of which the same could be said. They bear about a blighted vitality which the romance-writers call a broken heart.

But we are looking merely at the sad side of the convalescent. There are many happy little scenes to be seen about. Men who have long lain on beds of pain, who for the first time in months have wandered out under the summer sky and sniffed the strong odor of the budding trees and blooming flowers. One almost envies these fellows the superior beauties they perceive in nature's show. Others are being visited by friends and talking hopefully of going out soon and resuming their places amongst the toiling sons of men.

CHAPTER XXXI.
INFANT WAIFS.

Below the glittering surface of our beautiful civilization, drifting in the silent undertide is a current of guilt, injustice, and despair that has no voice to proclaim its misery. But its contagion affects the highest crest of the uplifted wave. The beings who dwell in these sunless depths of ignorance have been reached by no humanizing influences, and when events drive them into companionships that are new, with their imperfectly developed natures, the results cannot be otherwise than disastrous. It is from such conditions as these that the majority of our "unfortunates" and criminals come, and all the philosophic sentimentalism of the age cannot render a better account for them. With no means, so far known in this beneficent age, of staying this mighty current, the victims must be waited for near the bank of the whirlpool into which they are sooner or later destined to plunge in their mad career. For this kindly helpful purpose houses of reception, lying-in hospitals, and infant asylums are built and supported by civic and national governments, and benevolent, tender hearted men and women, of high social standing, give their time and attention to the management and direction of these institutions.

The infant asylums and houses of refuge in Toronto are many, and the most important ones are large and commodious. From the windows of one of these fall the softest, mellowest light, for lamps are shaded and turned low so as not to disturb the innocent sleepers. There are sixty children in the house all less than two years old. Some are in the arms of their mothers, some are in charge of some other unfortunate, and others lie in their little cots alone. Here is one resting as balmily as if the angel of household love and prosperity had presided at his birth instead of the darkness of disgrace and guilt. His cheeks are round and full and flushed with

THE WARM ROSE HUE OF SLEEP,

delicate eyelids cover great blue eyes, and the golden lashes lie like silken fringes on the soft face. Hair long and curling, the color of a buttercup is tossed from a fine high forehead, and a shapely tiny hand and rounded arm is thrust from under the cotton coverlet. He is strangely out of keeping with his surroundings, this lovely cherub boy, for he would grace the finest linen and silken hangings of a princely couch. Happier still he should have formed the golden nucleus of a home about which all the sweet domestic virtues might have bloomed.

Other little ones look curiously up with half closed eyes and drop to sleep again, but a wide-awake small boy lifts his dull eyes towards the matron and stretches out his weary arms for sympathy. In response the matron bestows upon him a wooden caress that is wholly unsatisfactory to the child. Soon the tired eyelids will have closed over all the tired eyes, and save for an occasional small cry the dormitory is quiet for the night, and the nurse in charge sleeps without serious interruption.

At midnight, sometimes, there is a ringing of the door-bell, a loud peremptory clangor. The matron goes down, draws the bolts, opens, and finds a policeman with a small parcel in his arms, or a basket in his hand.

"Oive brought yez an addition to the family, mum," says the man of the baton, and he recites the street and number where the infant was found. The child is perhaps a few days old, has the scantiest of clothing, indeed its entire wardrobe may consist of a strip of an old woolen shawl wrapped around and around it, and it is pretty sure to be drugged into a stupidity from which it takes some days to recover, and many of them die of the narcotics. And thus this silent, despairing, dumb under-current manifests its existence to the world. The mothers of the children that fill foundling and orphan asylums are from the most ignorant classes. They are not of the women of the town, compared with whom they are relatively innocent. Many of them are farm servants, and numbers of them are immigrants unable to speak the English language. Of the mothers of the foundlings nothing is positively known; every suspicion is founded on conjecture. If the child is ever taken by its parents it is by adoption.

The mothers who present themselves with a child in arms, and just from the hospital, have to pass a board of inspectors for admission to the home. They are required to remain in the institution six months, and each

TO NURSE A MOTHERLESS ONE

beside her own or take charge of a run-about child. When the mother goes away she usually leaves the child and pays a weekly sum for its maintenance or makes it over to managers, who offer it for adoption.

A great many, most of the children who are taken to asylums of this sort, become candidates for adoption. The work of disposing the waifs in suitable homes is one of intense interest and anxious responsibility. The adoption committee is composed, therefore, of the most efficient managers in the board. Members of this committee come into contact with no end of queer people and have many strange experiences to relate. The whole business is the outcome of the criminal side of life these papers are discussing, and as such these incidents are not incongruous here.

There are so many people and so many different sorts of people desiring children for adoption that it requires a peculiarly shrewd faculty and a practical knowledge of human nature to discriminate between the worthy and the unworthy. The circumstances of all persons wishing to adopt children are fully investigated, and references as to their respectability must be presented and approved before a child is committed to their care. Persons moving into new neighborhoods often intend passing the child as their own. Strange orders are often received from a distance—"special commissions," as manufacturers say. The child must have eyes of peculiar cerulean blueness, hair of a particular golden color, fingers tapering, nails pink-tinted, toes graduated to a nicety, and the limbs dimpled. There is not a doubt but that scores of happy new mothers could furnish just such a wonderful babe, but this order comes to the matron and managers of an infant asylum. A woman writes for a baby with brown, curly hair and large dark blue eyes, and a man—but how should he know any better?—telegraphs for a child with light curly hair, warranted to turn dark as the child grows older—the hair, mind you. During a year not more than three or four children with dark hair and eyes are called for, whereas people are anxious to get blonde girls, and many applications are made for children of that description. It looks as if it would take a strong revolution of popular feeling to restore brunettes to popular favor.

Certain it is, these good people would not be so fastidious if they got up their own babies. The greater number of people who take children from asylums are

CHILDLESS COUPLES

well on in life. A few children are adopted by widowers or widows. Some are taken by those kind-hearted, unselfish bodies who want something animate to love; others replace the loss of a dear little one by installing in its stead one of these little waifs. However, there are children enough for all whose hearts have mother love to lavish upon them.

Oftentimes the foundling asylum, in its general material capacity, is a very angel bringing peace and good will to discontented, childless couples, and sending happiness to distracted homes. An instance of its good work in this mission occurred in a city not a thousand miles from Toronto. Late one night a private carriage drove to the residence in a fashionable portion of the city, of one of the trustees of an asylum. A woman alighted, passed into the house, and secured an interview with the lady trustee. The visitor gave first-class references, and by all her outward manifestations was a person of wealth, and she looked as if she would require the services of Sairy Gamp in a few days.

"I am fooling the whole of them," she said, after some preliminary explanations. "I have been married some years, and am childless, and I am sure that my husband, who is now in Europe, will desert me on his return. His affections are completely alienated from me."

"But what can I do," exclaimed the trustee.

"Let me have an infant from the asylum to pass on him as my own. I will settle $20,000 a year on it when it comes of age."

The trustee told the would-be mother she would look her out in the morning and consult the other members of the committee. And the woman departed well satisfied with the result of her visit.

Next day her statements were all verified. She was found to be in easy circumstances, and in every way capable of taking care of a child.

So with the help of the hospital physician a pretty little girl, whose young mother on the night of its birth said she did not care what became of the nasty brat, was selected and the anxious mother was provided with a baby. No one but the Hospital doctor, the lady trustee and the "mother" knows the particulars of the dark transaction. The husband returned and went almost wild with delight. A few months later the trustee and the doctor were invited to visit the child. They found it lying in a satin-lined cradle, ornamented with blue ribbon and a white dove atop of the lace canopy.

"We are the happiest family in the world; my husband thinks there is nothing good enough for me and that child," is the testimony of the foster parent. The neatest part of the deception was that her mother-in-law was in the house when the child arrived and has never had a suspicion of its genuineness. Here is an instance where the delusion is practiced on the mother herself: There are mothers who lose all memory and mind when their infants are still-born, and go immediately into a slow fever, from which they do not recover for many months. There was a case of this sort in one of the most palatial of our city residences not long ago, and when it was known that the fifth child was dead, the husband brought a child from an institution, and placed it in its stead. The mother is transported with joy over her live child. She does not wish to be told that the babe she loves so much is not her own. She has her doubts, but she does not wish them confirmed.

CHAPTER XXXII.
THE PRETTY BOY.

There is a section of the young men in the city who may well be included in the ranks of the vicious classes. A deal of their miserable little histories is made during the hours of the night. These are the young men who live and fatten on their families. One may have some admiration for the brute courage of a man who takes the risk of death for the sake of ill-gotten gains of any kind. But what respect can we have for the thing that escapes labor by sticking like a barnacle to the hardly-earned comforts of a home on the strength of an affection that is all one-sided—that takes everything and gives nothing. But there is a class of young men in the city who do this. Fellows whom you see hanging about in the daytime, doing anything else but making an honest living, and whom you will find at night in improper places at all hours. One has no patience in writing about these fellows. They are the sons of men who have to work hard to make a livelihood, but in this latter particular the sons take good care not to imitate their sires. Probably every other member of the family contributes to the support of the decencies and comforts of the home except this drone, who is his mother's darling, and who is

TOO PRETTY TO BE SPOILED

on any mechanical work, and has not brains enough to do anything else. He sees his sisters go out every morning to earn a pittance which they ungrudgingly throw into the general funds at the close of each week, to the end that this loafer may be clothed in tight pants, a diagonal jacket and a fawn-colored overcoat, wherewith he may stand at a corner at nights and insult other men's sisters. One has no patience writing of this jackanapes. He is not generally a hard drinker. If he were to get drunk he would disarrange the sweet little love-locks that are oiled down over his retreating forehead. His greatest ambition is to make a mash on some indecent woman whose worst crime is her bad taste in bestowing caresses on such a creature. If her affection is of sufficient intensity to stand his bleeding her of her filthy gains, his joy is complete. The first use he makes of his beauty-money is to hire a furnished room in a public building where he plays the spider while silly young girls play the flies.

It is really extraordinary the length of time it takes for this thing to exhaust the affection of his family. The old man generally kicks pretty early in the game, but the barnacle simply ignores anything short of the old man's cowhide boots. His effrontery is amazing. Shame is a feeling unknown to him. He is a pretty boy, and it is the duty of all his relatives to preserve him in his pristine loveliness. He does not live in his home. He simply uses it. It is the

ONLY PURE PLACE HE ENTERS

and it is therefore uncongenial to him. All services rendered to him he takes as a matter of course, and as the natural homage which these inferior creatures, his mother and sisters (mere women) should pay to their handsome relative. He has no belief in the general purity of woman, but hears it impugned by the scurvy canaille with whom he associates without a chivalric blush for the gentle women at home to whom his swinish passions would not be understood. He is too much of a coward to commit crime and take chances of the penitentiary. When the day comes that his indignant father will stand him no longer, and kicks him out of doors, the choice of working, stealing, or starving is presented to him. He may steal now, often with a view to revenging himself on the people who have stood his disgraceful idleness so long. He will do anything that is dirty, or mean, or unprincipled rather than work, and the eternal justice is served when the penitentiary that fairly yearns for him scoops him in.

The only thing that he is regular in is his meals, and he doesn't come to them when he can get any outsider to pay for one for him.

HE TAKES IN EVERYTHING.

He may be found at horse-races, in billiard-rooms, at cock-fights, at street corners, at hotel doors—and everywhere he is in the way. He has seldom any money in his pocket, and as he must have good clothes, he spends a deal of his time endeavoring to discover tailors who don't know him, and who put trust in his nickel-plated promises.

This is the most pronounced type of the genus well-dressed loafer, but there are grades. Some work a little, others work a good deal—all spend everything they make on themselves, and exist at the expense of hard-working fathers, mothers, or sisters.

CHAPTER XXXIII.
WHAT'S IN A NAME?

The reporter makes gossip a business. He knows all the news of the city that is published, and he knows a good deal more that is never published. He asks you when he meets you, "Well, is there anything new?" and expects that you will disgorge all that you have heard that day, even if it concerns a matter that for your own interest had better not obtain publicity. He will think you a very mean man if you conceal from him the fact that your daughter has run away with the milkman, that you yourself have had a quarrel with your wife because she preferred the society of a man who carried a blue bag over his shoulder to that of her husband, or that you are short in your accounts and intend emigrating that night to a land of more salubrious climate than this. If you have had the misfortune to undergo any of these unpleasantnesses, or even others of lesser moment, the inquiring man of letters will feel utterly disgusted and aggrieved if you refuse to let him pluck the heart out of your mystery. If, however, you get the start of him and put the inquiry, "anything fresh?" you have got him. He will probably betray his chagrin by replying that the freshest thing he has seen that day is yourself, or employ some other threadbare witticism to cover his defeat. He will do anything but disclose to you his budget of facts. He probably has in his notebook things that will make the hair on the scalp of the great-headed public stand on end when his paper is issued and strewn broadcast among the people, but no word will he breathe to you of them. He knows that you would tell the first person you met, and thus

SET THE NEWS FLYING

until a rival journalist "got on to it." When the news is actually made public through his paper, he has no further interest in it. It is a lemon that has been sucked, and has now no piquancy for him. This is his attitude towards the information he gleans that is published, but still more reticent is he in regard to what he does not publish. The reporter, bit by bit, loses, like the doctor and the lawyer, his faith in human nature. Like them he often gets glimpses in the back corners of people's characters, which back corners are as guiltily hidden from the eye of man as the favorite sultana of an eastern monarch. As he goes along the street he sees many men who know him not, but whom he knows well. He knows of certain facts concerning them which the rest of the world knows nothing of. He sees them in places of honor and trust, in the mart, and in the church, and in the ball-room, and yet he knows that were those little damaging occurrences "learned by rote and cast into his teeth," the trader, the deacon and the partner in the dance would shun them like lepers and pass by on the other side. Many a reputation is saved by his leniency. One of his commonest experiences, next to requests to put in certain names in his paper, is requests to keep others out. Gentlemen who have had the misfortune to appear before the Magistrate in the morning are the most frequent attenders in reportorial rooms for this purpose. They have first made application to the reporter in the Police court, and he has referred them to the city editor. That gentleman generally asks, Why should the report be mutilated for the purpose of keeping your name out of the paper? He points out that the public pay their money for a paper with the understanding that all the city happenings that came under

THE REPORTER'S EYE

should be found recorded therein. The fact that you were discovered at two in the morning seated on a wood-pile, rocking a loose plank and singing hush-a-by-baby, evidently suffering from the hallucination that you were performing a sweet domestic duty, would be a very interesting item to serve up for the delectation of the people who live next door to you, and indeed to all those who know you. Now why should I rob them of that pleasure. Then the supplicant is heard as to why. If it is a first offence the city editor, following the Magistrate's rule, in all probability grants the prayer. This is the case of a man who has substantial standing in the community. But all kinds turn up on the same errand. A York street tough came in one day, and in a manner which was a curious blending of promises and threats, asked to have his name suppressed.

"You want your name kept out? Why it's been in our paper a dozen times for worse things than fighting. Go away boy, go away."

"Say, nobsy, I've got a new girl and she'll give me the shake if she sees that."

"Can't do it sir."

"Well, say, just make it read that I knocked the tar out o' Mulligan will you, and that'll make it all right."

Sometimes a clerk in an office or store creeks up the stairs and implores you for God's sake not to insert his name. He'll lose his situation, and when you agree to do so the gratitude that looks out of his watery eyes is unmistakable. The poor fellow, in spending a five dollar bill on his drunk, probably swallowed a whole week's salary, and has been thereby sufficiently punished. To this specimen the whole business possesses a ghastly seriousness, but there is another class who treat it as a huge joke. It has been noticed that men of this sort are usually Englishmen, and their desire to have their name omitted from the Police court roster has its rise in their fear of the ridicule of their fellows rather than any loss of character or position in consequence of its being made public.

and say they have been on "a bit of a spree and got lugged by a bobby," and ask in an off-hand way, "keep it hout will you, mistah," and sometimes "mistah" does.

Not quite a hundred years ago a man came into the presence of the city editor—tall, distinguished-looking man, clothed in the best West of England tweed. City editor very small person compared with man. Man takes chair offered him, and says, "I've got into a little scrape which you can help me out of if you would." City editor ought to feel flattered, that man would condescend to use him to help him out of a scrape. But he is very ungrateful and answers coldly: "How can I help you?"

"My wife," says the man "is one of the most unreasonable creatures in the world when she gets into a passion. I came home the night before last after having done a hard day's work in the store, and when I asked for a little supper she started to abuse me. She said a lot of mean things. I asked her to shut up for God's sake, and she wouldn't, and then, getting a little hot I tried to stop her tongue by putting the pillow on her head. That wouldn't have hurt a lamb, but she struggled so that she struck her head against the corner of the bed post and cut it. Then she ran out on the street, and she has disgraced me. A policeman got her, and as there was some blood on my wife's face he arrested me. I was bailed out immediately afterwards, but heavens, I had to appear in the court this morning. I don't care so much myself as for my wife and family. I am a subscriber and advertiser in your paper, and I hope you'll not say anything about it."

"Yes," said the city editor, "I have heard something about the case. You got home at half-past one and wanted your wife to get out of bed and cook you a steak. Some women are very unreasonable! After your working from ten in the morning until five at night, with only an hour for dinner! It was a shame. If she had only thought of the long time it took you to get home she would have had some idea how tired you were!"

"Well, sir, I didn't come here to be made a target for your humor. Where is the editor in chief?"

"You will find him down stairs, sir."

But the editor was out.

He is always "out" when cowardly cattle who beat their wives are around.

CHAPTER XXXIV.
THE SCARLET WOMAN.

The pickpocket who steals your watch, the burglar who invades your house in the middle of the night, or the foot-pad who knocks you down with a sand-bag, are citizens whom it is rather unpleasant to have any experience with, but it were better a thousand times to become the prey of any of these hawks of the night than that of those pitiless kites—the scarlet women of a great city. Against the thief the good burgher locks his doors and bars his windows, but these legionaries of passion assail a citadel where the master himself opens the gates and lets the insidious foe enter unopposed, if not with welcome.

Every city on this continent, not to speak of other lands at all, is afflicted with this army of iniquitous women. They form by far the largest section of the vicious classes in every great community of people. The evils they inflict on society, and the terrible consequences of their manner of life to themselves, temporally and spiritually, have constituted a theme for the moralist and a problem for the social reformer in all lands and in all ages.

Toronto, as has been before remarked in these sketches, is not a particularly wicked city. Few great crimes are perpetrated in our midst and but few great criminals claim this city as their home. But the fact that about 400 women openly live by a life of shame in this city speaks for itself. In the day time the public promenades are liberally sprinkled with

FLASHY FEMALES

arrayed in costly garments and costlier jewels. Beside these carrion birds of beauteous plumage the poor man's wife or daughter looks like a daw. Other forms of crime skulk in the daylight, coming forth only when the dark hours favor their calling, but these birds of prey hang out the signs of their nefarious calling at high noon, and strut the streets shaming the honest and demoralizing the weak. The girl who has worked all day until brain and fingers and limbs are tired, returning homewards at nightfall, compares her uneventful, dreary lot with the seemingly joyous existence of these women, looks at her own shabby gown and at their rich ones, and inwardly wonders if honesty, truth and worth are, after all, the best. The foolish youth who returns their smiles as he passes them on the pavement does not know that that little gloved hand is as cruel as the tiger's claws. That mother realized that the other day when she heard her eighteen-year-old boy doomed to wear the disgraceful livery of a convict. But her heartrending sobs did not ruffle a lace on the stony front of the fair-haired, showy enchantress, to buy whose mercenary caresses he had robbed his employer. He was a smooth-cheeked, good-looking, clean-limbed boy, with candor marked in every line of his face.

His deeds found no record in the straightforward look of his blue eyes. But drag him away from his mourning mother, policeman, and let him break his spirit among the other jail-birds. Let Circe go free and entice other boys into her toils. She didn't know he was stealing the goods—no, not she. Yes, let her go free, but before she goes to sleep each night let her think of a room wherein another woman stands in

DUMB, TEARLESS AGONY,

before the picture of her son. Let there be no desire, however, to lessen that son's infamy who forgot a mother's love and a sister's devotion for the smiles of a harlot.

"There is a great deal of soft-hearted nonsense talked about these women of the town," said a gentleman connected with the Society for the Prevention of Vice. "My firm conviction is that not one in ten is deserving of any more sympathy than we give to other criminals. People talk about men's brutal instincts and women's weakness, but a long experience and a good deal of thought on the subject has brought me the conclusion that not one quarter of the bad women of this city have drifted into their present lives through deceit on the part of men. What I mean to say is that in the fall of the majority of those women they had an equal share of sin with the men."

"Oh, you take a cynical view of the matter. You know well the lengths to which some men will go to accomplish their purposes. They seize some weak point in their victim and work upon that. If they capture her affections under promise of marriage they accomplish their purpose. If she is fond of dress or ornaments the rich libertine captures her by rich presents."

"You might as well excuse a thief on the same grounds. If a girl went into a store and

STOLE A HANDSOME BONNET

or a fine pair of boots you wouldn't pardon her, would you, because she was fond of handsome bonnets or fine boots. In regard to being deceived by men, I grant you that I know personally of some cases where women have fallen through the machinations of villains—been brought to evil by devilish, calculating, cold-blooded deceit. But I am certain that the numbers of these in proportion to the others is very small indeed. But even these, apart from the evil involved in their very struggle for existence, work wickedness from the promptings of a heart which very fast becomes hard and impressionless as marble. I tell you, if there is any sympathy to be wasted on either, it is to be given to the victims of these harridans. Let them once get their clutches on a man, and they will hold him there until they have plucked him bare, and until he hasn't enough character left to dust a tumbler with."

"I am afraid the discussions of your society have swamped your charity."

"I have as much charity as most people, but what I do say is that the social evil can't be cured by petting and sympathy alone. Of course, in the present condition of things, you can't put in force those

REPRESSIVE MEASURES

which I believe to be the only way in which the evil can be permanently lessened. You can't start driving girls out of the houses they have to cover them without providing some way in which they can get food and shelter. But, sir, I am convinced that the way to cut off the supply of recruits is to make life in a bagnio unpleasant, unprofitable, and less seductive. Anyhow, by all means keep these flaming women off the streets. That does more to attract light-headed, vain girls into the ranks than any other one thing. I believe this could be done very easily. Just intimate gently that any house whose inmates were constantly parading the streets in their war-paint was liable to be raided, and I tell you this promenading would stop suddenly."

"Now, have you any clear idea how the social evil might be wiped out?"

"I don't believe it can be wiped out while the world lasts, but what I do believe is that if the matter were taken hold of with courage it could be lessened and rendered less attractive to weak girls. I admit that even this is quite a difficult thing to accomplish. You would not believe the amount of sympathy that exists in high places for these women. You would have to encounter and defeat all that and trample on a score of prejudices, but the man or body of men who tackle the subject and deal with it boldly and wisely will

SAVE MANY A GIRL

from a miserable life ending in all probability in a miserable death. My leading thoughts about the whole business is that our kindness and consideration for the women already ruined is cruelty to certain classes of our females. Better be hard on the erring than be neglectful of the influences and examples that surround those who are as yet uncorrupted."

"What did you accomplish by the repressive measures put in force some eighteen months ago?"

"There are others could answer that better than I can. I was out of town for a while after the campaign was at its height. But I have been told that the streets at least were free from the presence of the women. A gentleman told me that he knew of three cases where keepers of houses had abandoned the business and had been living quietly ever since. But I wish you would see people who know more about this than I do."

CHAPTER XXXV.
BEHOLD, THERE MET HIM A WOMAN.

The News man sought a clergyman who is well-known for his zeal and earnest preaching, which excuses him in the eyes of many, at least, for his somewhat heterodox views. He was asked to give his ideas with regard to the expediency of treating such a subject as the social evil in the public prints in the interest of morality. Without hesitation he picked up a Bible.

"Here," he said, "is what a greater and wiser than I has said on that subject, and though I would not be forgiven, perhaps, if I spoke so plainly, yet these words of the sage of Israel should command respect and excite the people to a greater activity in repressing this terrible social blight. Here is what we find in the 7th chapter of Proverbs:"

"For at the window of my house I looked through my casement, and beheld among the simple ones, I discerned among the youths, a young man void of understanding passing through the street near her corner. And he went the way to her house in the twilight, in the evening, in the black and dark night.

And, behold, there met him a woman with the attire of an harlot, and subtil of heart.

She is loud and stubborn. Her feet abide not in her house.

Now is she without, now in the streets, and lieth in wait at every corner.

So she caught him, and kissed him, and with an impudent face said unto him, I have peace offerings with me. This day have I payed my vows.

Therefore came I forth to meet thee, diligently to seek thy face, and I have found thee.

I have decked my bed with coverings of tapestry, with carved works, with fine linen of Egypt.

I have perfumed my bed with myrrh, aloes and cinnamon.

Come, let us take our fill of love until the morning; let us solace ourselves with loves.

For the goodman is not at home, he is gone a long journey.

He hath taken a bag of money with him, and will come home at the day appointed.

With her much fair speech she caused him to yield, with the flattering of her lips she forced him.

He goeth after her straightway, as an ox goeth to the slaughter, or as a fool to the correction of the stocks. Till a dart strike through his liver, as a bird hasteth to the snare, and knoweth not that it is for his life.

Hearken unto me now therefore, O ye children, and attend to the words of my mouth.

Let not thine heart incline to her ways, go not astray in her paths.

For she hath cast down many wounded; yea, many strong men have been slain by her.

Her house is the way of hell, going down to the chambers of death."

"These words were written about two thousand years ago by Solomon, the son of David, the king of Israel. The lapse of centuries has not abated a jot of their truth. No other part of holy writ contains plainer or more terrible warnings than gleam from these verses. Solomon, the wisest man of Israel, evidently did not hold with the doctrine that it is better that these matters should be quietly ignored, let the cancer

EAT INTO SOCIETY

rather than apply the knife. It is a foul thing, therefore let it fester and corrupt, rather than expose it to the physician's eye. The physician cannot eradicate altogether, therefore let him not even try to confine its ravages. There are many who hold these views, and their opinions are entitled to respect; and it behoves you to explain the motives by which you are actuated and the practical purposes at which you aim in your present inquiry. An explanation of this kind is called for inasmuch as the subject treated of has seldom been urged upon the public attention or exhibited in all its painful associations. This being the case it would be no matter of wonder if in some instances your work should meet with an unwelcome reception. The human mind, when it has long been familiar with an existing evil, comes at last contentedly to endure, and will even behold with a jealous eye any attempt, however well-meant, that would threaten to overthrow it. The apathy which has been so generally manifested regarding the social evil cannot be accounted for except on some such principle as this. For it is a lamentable fact that while the sympathies of the public have been awakened, their exertions drawn forth, and their resources liberally applied in promoting other philanthropic schemes having for their object the alleviation of human suffering and the positive advancement of the moral and physical well-being of the species, this mystery of iniquity, more ruinous in its tendencies and more fearfully disastrous in its effects than any other kind of crime, has in a great measure been overlooked."

"Many individuals disapprove altogether of any publication of this kind on the ground that the disclosures necessary to be made are apt to minister to an already vitiated taste or to

FAMILIARIZE THE MINDS

of the young and inexperienced with subjects that have a tendency to mislead or deprave them. Suppose this argument were admitted to have some force, what, it may be asked, is to be done with a system so debasing in its nature and so ruinous in its results? Is it better to suffer it to go on perpetuating itself and contentedly to behold it carrying down its thousands to a gloomy grave than to make a determined effort to resist its progress, simply because such an effort may, perhaps, minister to a vitiated appetite or exert a deceitful influence on the mind of some thoughtless youth? Even on the supposition that some wretched man may be rendered more miserable, or some hopeful youth may have his moral principles shaken, still the evil to be remedied is of so gigantic a nature that its arrestment would not be too dearly purchased, were the supposed consequences necessarily connected with it. But it may, after all, be a question whether such an idea be not visionary. Would a disclosure that could be offered with any degree of consistency to the public, tend to deprave still more the taste of that man who has already abandoned himself to sensual gratifications, and who is in the daily practice of associating with persons whose actions and habits constitute the very essence of impurity? Or is a man who has partially gone astray, but who still retains some sensibility of moral sentiment, likely to make a more rapid descent when his path is seen to be strewed with the melancholy remains of human victims? Or shall it be affirmed that a youth—as yet uncontaminated with the vices of the world, and whose mind has been disciplined to soundness of thinking—would experience any other sensation than that of horror at the exhibition of human folly and guilt?

"THE NEWS" he concluded "should consider its labor well bestowed, and its exertions amply rewarded if through its instrumentality, the public shall be made to think more seriously and to act more vigorously in regard to a subject which I consider of infinite moment, connected as it is with the everlasting destiny of no inconsiderable portion of the human race."

CHAPTER XXXVI.
KILLJOY HOUSE.

The French in their superficial way speak of a bagnio as a maison de joie, which may be translated literally as a house of joy. It would be impossible to conceive of a more false description of these habitations of vice. Riotous exhilaration produced by drink there is, hideous hysterical hilarity there is—but joy, none. The merriment of the inmates of such a house has a commercial value, and they do not use any of it when the men who pay for it are not about.

"I have often thought," said a man who was connected with the city police for some ten years, a man of great good sense and wide general reading, "that the people who speak in condemnation of the social evil do not dwell sufficiently on the actual revolting facts connected with the life of a woman of the town. I have read sensational newspaper articles, and I have heard preachers' sermons on the subject, but in all there is a lack of practical treatment. After you have read or heard them, a person who does not know the facts would think that a house of ill-fame was the abode of wicked and unholy but yet picturesque passion. In spite of themselves they succeed in surrounding the unsavory mess with a halo of romance, than which there could be nothing further from the facts. There is no romance in the lives of evil women. Everything about them is gross, sordid and mercenary. The master passion of their lives is not sensuality, but a greed for money and display conjoined with envy and all uncharitableness. They are the slaves of the vile women who keep the houses in which they live. While they are new to the life, pretty and popular, they are allowed certain latitude. These are the ones whom you see parading the streets, sitting in the houses of entertainment, and driving to the races. But when

THEIR WITHERING LIVES

begin to tell upon their good looks, their days of merriment are over. They now become slaves in the vilest sense of the word. The money for which they sell their souls is the constant prey of the hoary old brothel-keeper to whom they are in bondage. The majority of the men who visit their dens are in liquor. Is there anything picturesque about half-a-dozen dull-eyed creatures being roused out of their sleep in the small hours of the morning to be marshalled before an old brute with rum-laden breath and filthy person whose sottish fancy has led him here? Is it possible to conceive a woman with a single vestige of pride left consenting to be at the pick and choose of such a loathsome creature? Yet this is a frequent sight in these houses of hell. Is there any romance about that? And when the choice is made the other five are eaten with envy. But it is envy, spitefulness, and all uncharitableness, morning, noon and night with them. The demon of hatred is the presiding spirit of their sunless habitations. She who has good looks and youth is a continual eyesore to the woman whose lustre of girlhood is a thing now of memory. She is hated and slandered, and she glories in the fact because it is a tribute to qualities which she has that they have not. But her hour comes too soon and too surely, and a younger rival hurries her down the slope, to be herself displaced in turn as the months go by, leaving their impress of dissipation.

Envy and hatred of each other are common characteristics, and the same may be said of lying, intemperance and profanity. Lying is part of their trade, and is a necessity of their existence, and so much of a habit does the practice become that they

LIE BY PREFERENCE.

If the truth were equally profitable, they would lie by choice. I have often heard them relate the stories of their lives to officers of charities or prisons, and in almost all cases the statements were wildly improbable. One of them spoke of being of good family and having been educated in a convent, when it was discovered that she could neither read nor write. The story of their downfall, as told by themselves, is always attributed to being the result of loving not wisely, but too well. In many cases I have heard this claim made, when the men in the force knew the whole history of the dame, and knew her representations to be absurdly false."

"Well, you don't mean to say that in your experience you haven't met women who owed their downfall to the seductive wiles of men."

"I am only speaking of these women in the aggregate, and giving you their general characteristics. I look upon them all as unfortunate, and some more so than others. Some deserve the description of unfortunates in the same degree as the burglars and thieves in the prisons do. Others undoubtedly are led into the life by a cruel fate. Indeed I know of such a case. Five years ago there lived near me a family, consisting of a husband and wife, and a son and daughter. The husband was a useless old moke, who didn't even have energy enough to get drunk, but his wife had, and did. The boy, who was the eldest of the two children, was a rough, and got into a fight aboard an excursion boat, and came near killing a man. He fled to the States, and as far as I know has never been heard of in this city since. Mary was the only one of the family for whom the neighbors had any respect. She was a shy girl and seemed to

KNOW NOTHING BUT TO WORK

away at an old sewing machine, making overalls for a factory. Any time that Mary was seen outdoors was carrying great big bundles wrapped in a brown piece of linen, which she brought back full of work, and was seen no more till that dole of labor was completed. The neighbors tolerated the family on Mary's account. Mary's dress was about as uninteresting as the brown lining which invariably encircled her work, but those who look for beauty unadorned saw in her dark eyes and delicate complexion things that were pleasant to look upon. But the chief glory of humble little Mary was her brown hair, which fairly flowed in a cataract down her back. She was very much ashamed of these unruly locks, and when she went abroad they were tucked away in as small a knot as they could be squeezed into at the back of her head. But people caught glimpses of them at odd times, and the fame of Mary's ringlets spread abroad on the street.

Suddenly there came a change in her ways. She commenced to exhibit some coquetry in dress. But I need not weary you with the details of her decline and fall. Suffice it to say that Mary was missed from home one day and her mother bewailed in her cups that her daughter had gone to the bad.

One night I was standing in the shadow of a lamp on Elizabeth street when a woman came along. I knew Mary and stopped her. She exhibited great fear and shame-facedness but I talked to her and finally gained her confidence. She was very anxious to know what the neighbors thought of her. "They are very sorry that you have forgot yourself, Mary," I answered. "I had to do it," she said. I tried to reach the meaning of this answer but it was only after a long time that she told me her story. She told in a singularly simple and feeling way

HER STORY.

"I am awfully sorry Mr. — for what has happened, but I couldn't help it. My feelings were stronger than myself. There was something happened one day that changed all my life. You remember the bundles I used to carry. Well, one day, when I was on my way home it started to rain, and before I went two blocks I was soaking. Just then a car overtook me, and I hailed it. I was never on a car before, but I had money that I had just got from my boss, and I thought I could afford it. I struggled into the car with my wet bundle. There were six ladies and three gentlemen in the car. There was plenty of room for me on either side if they had sat closer, but not one of them moved. I stood there like a fool till one of the gentlemen at the far end of the car stood up and asked me to take his seat. When I went to sit down, the lady who had sat close enough to him, drew as far away from me as possible. I never before felt what a dowdy ill-dressed thing I was, but I thought so then. My face was crimson, and I could not look up for the world. Oh, how I wished I had never got on that car. It became unbearable at length, and I made a foolish attempt to get off the car before ringing the bell, and I fell on one of the ladies, and she was very indignant. The gentleman who had given me his seat picked up my bundle and carried it out, while I slunk out after him wishing that the earth would swallow me. He carried my bundle to the sidewalk and asked me which way I was going. I told him, and then when he found I had got off the car long before I was near my home, he laughed at me, and joked about the way the old cats (that's what he called them) had treated me. That adventure was the

TURNING POINT OF MY LIFE.

That man's appearance and voice and smile have haunted me to my ruin. I thought him a god, and when I considered that he took my part before all those ladies I would willingly have let him tramp on me or kill me. A blow from that man would have been sweeter a thousand times than the smiles of another. He did not lose sight of me. I could refuse him nothing and he was but too ready to use his power over me. What is the use of talking. You see what I am.

"Now, sir," continued my friend "the man who ruined this girl is what I call a professional masher. He still exists to ply his arts. That was as fine a girl as ever lived, and she was led away by her better instincts, either love or gratitude, I don't exactly know which. But I think this is an exceptional case. The great majority go astray from pure cussedness. Love of dress, indolence, licentiousness, and bad temper will be found to have more to do with the propagation of the social evil than man's perfidy and woman's weakness."

"Your views are very like those of another gentleman I interviewed—all in favor of the men."

"I haven't said a word in favor of the men. I loathe the men who consort with these women, especially the married portion of them. When I was a policeman I became acquainted with the dirty habits of many of this class, and I felt so angry with them that when I would meet them going along the street during the day with their sanctimonious faces I would feel like slapping them. No, sir; I don't defend the men, but neither do I want to see the woman held blameless when she deliberately chooses this life, and by her example corrupts and entraps others. But I started out to talk about the grossness of life in a bagnio, and here I have been telling stories, but that's your own fault in interrupting me. I was looking for a thief one night when I was acting-detective. I found out where his "woman" lived, and I felt sure the way to catch him was to

WATCH WHERE SHE LIVED.

The house was neither first nor second-class, but a compromise between the two. It got very cold, and after loitering about for an hour, and getting chilled to the bone, I concluded I could watch inside as well as out. My only fear was that some of the inmates would recognize who I was. I took chances, however, and rang the bell. I was admitted without much trouble. I found that the greater number of the inmates of the house were much under the influence of liquor. There were three men in the room into which I was shown. Each had a woman seated on his knee. Three more came tripping down stairs, the first of whom threw herself into my lap and encircled my neck with her arms. I cannot say her attentions were appreciated. A sickening odor of stale beer permeated her person, and she was decidedly drunk. The other two who had come down stairs with her were not so bad, but they were evidently inclined to be sarcastic about the suddenness of her attack on me. They evidently thought she should have given me a chance to make my pick. I was anxious to find out which was the "woman" of the man I was in search of, and when the nymph who occupied my knee asked me to buy a bottle of beer I complied, the more willingly as it relieved me of her unpleasant bulk and

ODORIFEROUS BREATHINGS.

The beer was brought and I was assessed $1 for it. During its consumption I discovered the woman I wanted. A very brief conversation with her showed me that she was expecting some other society than mine that evening. "Don't be making up to me," she said. "I expect a 'friend,' and the landlady would raise Cain if I threw business for him."

I felt pretty certain that my thief would show up shortly. By this time the drunkest of the three who had come down stairs on my entrance, was quarreling with the others and threatening all sorts of dire disasters. The profanity and sewer-talk was something frightful. At last one of them struck her with a glass, and in a moment there was a frightful commotion. There was no fight in the poor, drunken creature, and the sight of the blood which flowed from her brow frightened her into maudlin tears. She sat on the floor, while the blood dabbled her white night-dress, and rocked back and fore, moaning "Cora, I didn't think you'd stab me."

After this incident, although I saw no more drinking in the room, I observed that each time they re-appeared they were all getting drunker and drunker. The landlady of the house, a coarse, scowling woman, tried to keep them quiet, but they sang snatches of song, and swore, and quarreled, and blows were ever and anon freely interchanged. It was a scene I can neither describe nor forget, and I was overjoyed in more ways than one when I saw Pearl, who was the only one who was anyways sober, go to the door and return with my man. I had the handcuffs on him before he recovered from his surprise. When it was known that an arrest had been made in the house, there was a great hubbub. Women rushed here and there like demented things, and I took advantage of this consternation to slip out with my prisoner. Again, I say, that there is not one tinge of romance, sentiment or any other ennobling thing about the lives of evil women. There is no passion, not even sensuality on the part of the woman, nothing but a dirty account of bargain and sale, that one of the parties to the transaction may compound with a rapacious brothel-keeper for her lodgings and semi-occasional meals."

With this remark my friend moved away.

CHAPTER XXXVII.
LEADING DOWN TO DEATH.

It is seldom possible to watch the whole career of an abandoned woman. As they step lower and lower in abasement they keep moving from city to city until they reach a stage where the next descent must be into the grave. It is, therefore, difficult to trace their progress, from the "high-toned" fast house to the hospital pallet where they finish a life of loathsomeness by a still more loathsome death.

It has been calculated that the average span of existence for a woman who embraces a life of shame does not average more than five or six years. A year of the irregular life suffices to seriously impair that youth and their good looks, and then they begin to experience the bitterness and the hatefulness of the terrible trade which they have launched themselves. The extravagance and improvidence of their natures soon put them completely in the power of the soulless harridan who keeps the house. She contrives that they shall always be owing her money. She has good security in their wardrobes, and their lives from this time out become one long struggle with debt, hatred of the landlady who oppresses them, ill-health, and disease.

Information derived from many quarters shows with unmistakeable distinctness

THE AWFUL PUNISHMENTS

which follow hard upon the heels of the sin of unchastity. Interviews with medical men set forth a state of affairs the recital of which beggars language to give it due utterance. All that is horrible in human misery and possible in physical debility and degradation visits the bodies of these poor outcasts of the earth.

"When I was a young man," said a physician to the writer, "I used to think that if a woman who had just taken her first step in infamy were to visit certain of the wards in the great hospitals and see the masses of living putrescence, which were once fair women, who are there rotting away on their last couches, the sight would serve to drive them back into the paths of rectitude and virtue, though all other argument on earth would fail to do so. Doctors get used to terrible sights, but the venereal ward of an hospital never ceases to shock and disgust. No amount of use can make the physician on each recurring visit less sensible of the overwhelming calamity that has overtaken these hapless victims of brutal lust."

So certain are these terrible consequences to ensue on a life of shame, that women of this class seldom put in a year of the life without contracting one or other of the dreadful diseases which afflict and pursue them to the grave.

Their time is spent between the bagnio and the hospital, and each recurrence of their disorders makes them more and more whited sepulchres, moving like an incarnate plague, dealing out poisoned contamination to their guilty male associates, a contamination that confirm in a striking way the terrible dictum of scripture, that the sins of the father shall be visited on the children unto the third and fourth generation. Verily "Her house is the way of hell, leading down to the chambers of death."

No matter what opinion may be entertained with regard to the proper methods of

LESSENING THE EVILS OF PROSTITUTION

it is impossible to witness the downward course of its victims without regret and pity. Even in cases where the life has been chosen with the utmost deliberation from the worst of motives, it is but natural that the condign punishment that surely awaits the modern Magdalen should awaken our sympathy, and kindle in the philanthropic mind a desire to turn out of the road of such calamity the erring feet of wilful women. It is not the purpose of these sketches to preach. The aim has been merely to point out what exists in our midst, and leave public opinion in its aggregate wisdom to settle the problems which these facts present. Every right-thinking person must sympathize with the efforts that Christian men and women make to rescue this class from their lives of sin. The legislators of the province in establishing the Mercer prison, dealt with the question both in a penal and reformatory spirit. Other lesser institutions have been founded by philanthropic persons entirely reformatory and helpful in their character. Of this nature are the Magdalen asylum and the Haven. Both of these undoubtedly do commendable work. The percentage of reformations effected is certainly small, but small as it is it encourages the willing workers to go on. Their chief endeavors should be directed towards eradicating from public sentiment the feeling that the woman who loses her honor

CAN NEVER CLIMB BACK

into respectability and forgiveness again.

This is the philanthropic aspect of the base. But it has another. It has its criminal aspect.

County Crown Attorney Fenton, who is the secretary of the Society for the Prevention of Vice, was asked what his society was doing in regard to the social evil.

"The society," he said, "is in statu quo at present. The gentlemen who compose it did what they could and got a great deal of help from the police commissioners but they could not get Major Draper into their way of thinking. Letters passed between the chief and me but nothing ever came of it. My last letter requested him to give me a list of the houses known to the police to be houses of ill fame, but this he refused to do on the ground that he did not know what use I was to make of the information."

Here Mr. Fenton laughed very heartily.

"What were the plans of the society for the eradication of the evil?"

"I don't think the society had any hope of wiping out the evil. All they hoped to do was to keep it in check. I know that my views were simply these. The law of the land declares that keeping a house of ill-fame, or being an inmate thereof, are offences punishable by

FINE AND IMPRISONMENT.

The chief constable and all his men are sworn to enforce the laws of the land, and I proposed they should do so in this particular class of cases."

"There were some raids made about that time. What were the results of them?"

"Well, during the discussion of the question large numbers of the women took fright, and they left the city in droves. Quite a number were arrested when the raids were made, and a few sent to the Mercer, and more fined. Two or three keepers were frightened out of the business."

"Didn't the girls disappear off the public streets at that time?"

"Yes; I am told they did."

"But are they not now as bold and as numerous as ever there?"

"I really couldn't say. The society may give the subject its serious attention soon, and if it does, I'll endeavor to make it as hot for these 'high-toned' houses as for the more miserable ones."

The reporter could have told him that the public promenades are thronged these days with females exhibiting the richest fabrics which the shops afford.

CHAPTER XXXVIII.
ANOTHER CLASS OF PROMENADERS.

In another of these sketches I have spoken of certain members of the female sex who spend the most of their evenings in promenading the streets. They are young and full of lusty life. I come now to another class of promenaders—the saddest class of all God's creatures—hopeless, heartless. It is almost impossible to avoid sermonizing in dealing with this sisterhood of sin. They are treated enough to words of opprobrium and hate. Let them be spoken of here rather in pity than in anger, and when the awful lessons of their sins are ascertained and pointed out, let them sink into the obscurity out of which neither law, love, nor mercy seems sufficient to lift them.

"Good evening," said a woman to me one night as I was going to the Parliament buildings. The voice was harsh and hoarse. She passed as close to me as possible, but her tone implied that she would not be surprised if she got no answer. I was not in a hurry and I stopped.

"Do you want to see me?" I said.

She exhibited some signs of fear now. Probably she thought I was one of the brigade of the famous police mashers.

"No, I guess not," was the answer, as she peered inquiringly at me. "I was feeling lonesome and I just passed the time o' day."

"Feeling lonesome, eh; what makes you lonesome?"

"I'm lonesome because my fellah doesn't come along."

"Don't you feel cold?"

"A little chilly; but I know where we can be warm."

Ghastly humor! The little laugh with which it was accompanied raised

A FIT OF COUGHING,

which she vainly tried to control. It shook her shivering frame beneath the flimsy rags until she staggered on the sidewalk.

After the paroxysm had subsided I said, "That's a bad cough you have. Have you had it long?"

"Oh, no; I am as strong and good as ever I was. I got a little cold the other night," she said, as she placed her hand upon her thin breast in a vain endeavor to check another outburst.

If she had only known. That cough would prove a better extractor of coin from men's pockets than the disgusting arts of her wretched trade. Her physical frailties would appeal more to men's hearts than her withered and sickening leer. After some further conversation, which need not be repeated, I said:

"Cease being a curse to men, and a curse to yourself! Before you die, repent, and make peace with your Maker, whose image you disgrace."

She looked wonderingly for a moment, then cast her eyes to the earth.

"My God, sir, I must have a place to sleep to-night. If I sleep out another night it'll kill me."

If all the men and women of this land could have heard the despair in that woman's voice! A thousand maxims on virtue, a thousand sermons on sin could not produce the effect of these words wailed out in the night. This is the end of the "lark"—traversing the dismal streets, hawking about the very jewel of womanhood for the price of a ragged quilt and a covering from the skies.

The charity of a stranger gave her a bed for that night and for other nights.

There came a night when she didn't, and in the morning a group of laborers stood looking at a form huddled close against a fence. Her nails were full of sand, and the torn turf told the story of her agony as the purple blood from her lungs had gushed in great clots from her lips. Her face was pinched and drawn and the eyes stared awfully. The blood had flowed down her cheek and mingled amid the strands of her hair. A paragraph in the papers next day told that "the Mayor yesterday granted an order for the burial of the poor woman found on Garrison street." She had enacted the part chosen by her in life. She had been born and had found a grave.

THE END.

Milton Keynes UK
Ingram Content Group UK Ltd.
UKHW020832200524
442968UK00005B/601